DESIGNING PROFESSIONAL DEVELOPMENT
IN LITERACY

SOLVING PROBLEMS IN THE TEACHING OF LITERACY
Cathy Collins Block, *Series Editor*

Recent Volumes

Multicultural and Multilingual Literacy and Language: Contexts and Practice
Edited by Fenice B. Boyd and Cynthia H. Brock, with Mary Z. Rozendal

Teaching All the Children: Strategies for Developing Literacy in an Urban Setting
Edited by Diane Lapp, Cathy Collins Block, Eric J. Cooper, James Flood,
Nancy Roser, and Josefina Villamil Tinajero

Conceptual Foundations of Teaching Reading
Mark Sadoski

The Literacy Coach's Handbook: A Guide to Research-Based Practice
Sharon Walpole and Michael C. McKenna

Comprehension Process Instruction: Creating Reading Success in Grades K–3
Cathy Collins Block, Lori L. Rodgers, and Rebecca B. Johnson

Adolescent Literacy Research and Practice
Edited by Tamara L. Jetton and Janice A. Dole

Tutoring Adolescent Literacy Learners: A Guide for Volunteers
Kelly Chandler-Olcott and Kathleen A. Hinchman

Success with Struggling Readers: The Benchmark School Approach
Irene West Gaskins

Making Sense of Phonics: The Hows and Whys
Isabel L. Beck

Reading Instruction That Works, Third Edition: The Case for Balanced Teaching
Michael Pressley

Narrowing the Literacy Gap: What Works in High-Poverty Schools
Diane M. Barone

Reading Assessment and Instruction for All Learners
Edited by Jeanne Shay Schumm

Word Sorts and More: Sound, Pattern, and Meaning Explorations K–3
Kathy Ganske

Reading the Web: Strategies for Internet Inquiry
Maya B. Eagleton and Elizabeth Dobler

Designing Professional Development in Literacy: A Framework
for Effective Instruction
Catherine A. Rosemary, Kathleen A. Roskos, and Leslie K. Landreth

Designing
Professional Development
in Literacy

A FRAMEWORK
FOR EFFECTIVE INSTRUCTION

CATHERINE A. ROSEMARY
KATHLEEN A. ROSKOS
LESLIE K. LANDRETH

Foreword by Ronald Gallimore

THE GUILFORD PRESS
New York   London

Printed in the United States of America

This book is printed on acid-free paper.

Last digit is print number: 9 8 7 6 5 4 3 2 1

Library of Congress Cataloging-in-Publication Data
Rosemary, Catherine A.
    Designing professional development in literacy : a framework for effective instruction / Catherine A. Rosemary, Kathleen A. Roskos, Leslie K. Landreth; foreword by Ronald Gallimore.
        p. cm.—(Solving problems in the teaching of litercy)
    Includes bibliographical references and index.
    ISBN-13: 978-1-59385-430-0 ISBN-10: 1-59385-430-7 (pbk. : alk. paper)
    ISBN-13: 978-1-59385-431-7 ISBN-10: 1-59385-431-5 (cloth : alk. paper)
    1. Language arts (Primary)—United States.   2. Reading (Primary)—United States.   3. Effective teaching—United States.   I. Roskos, Kathy.   II. Landreth, Leslie K.   III. Title.
    LB1529.U5R67 2007
    372.41—dc22
                                                                            2006032057

About the Authors

Catherine A. Rosemary, PhD, is Associate Professor in the Department of Education and Allied Studies at John Carroll University in Cleveland, Ohio. Before joining the university in 1995, Dr. Rosemary worked for 16 years in public schools as a special education teacher, reading specialist, and director of curriculum and instruction. She currently directs the Literacy Specialist Project, a statewide professional development initiative for improving literacy teaching in preschools through grade 12, and is codirector of the Reading First—Ohio Center for Professional Development and Technical Assistance in Effective Reading Instruction. Her work has led to numerous research presentations and publications on the influence of professional development on teacher learning and practice. Dr. Rosemary was instrumental in developing the Literacy Specialist Endorsement, a newly offered credential available to teachers in Ohio.

Kathleen A. Roskos, PhD, a Professor in the Department of Education and Allied Studies at John Carroll University, teaches courses in reading instruction and reading diagnosis. Formerly an elementary classroom teacher, Dr. Roskos has served in a variety of educational administration roles, including director of federal programs in the public schools and department chair in higher education. For 2 years she directed the Ohio Literacy Initiative at the Ohio Department of Education, providing leadership in pre-K–12 literacy policy and programs. Dr. Roskos studies early literacy development and learning, teacher cognition, and the design of professional education for teachers, and has published research articles on these topics in leading journals. She is currently a member of the e-Learning Committee and the Early Childhood Commission of the International Reading Association (IRA) and President of the IRA's Literacy Development for Young Children Special Interest Group.

Leslie K. Landreth, MA, is Assistant Director of the Literacy Specialist Project at John Carroll University, where she also teaches undergraduate reading courses as an adjunct instructor. Before joining the Literacy Specialist Project in January 2000, she taught for 25 years in elementary schools and libraries in Michigan, California, South Carolina, and Ohio. Her work has been driven by a passion for children's literature, an interest in the English language, and a desire to provide effective literacy instruction. Ms. Landreth's current role with the Literacy Specialist Project centers on the design and implementation of a literacy curriculum for educators in Ohio. Through her curriculum development work, she has made significant contributions to statewide professional development in literacy.

Acknowledgments

No large-scale project is created and sustained without the dedication and hard work of colleagues, supporters, critics, fans, and friends. Many educators at many different levels helped to make the Literacy Specialist (LS) Project a reality in schools and contributed to the content of this book. We owe them all deep thanks.

For their creativity and abiding belief in the LS Project, we thank Jane Wiechel, Associate Superintendent of the Center for Students, Families, and Communities at the Ohio Department of Education, and Sandy Miller, Executive Director of the Office of Early Learning and School Readiness at the Ohio Department of Education. They were there with us at the genesis of the project and remain true to it still.

For their intellectual energy and considerable year-to-year effort, we thank our university partners who implement the LS Project in their local schools. We are grateful, especially, to our cofounders in those early, program-building days: Eileen Carr, University of Toledo; Joyce Feist-Willis, Youngstown State University; Penny Freppon, University of Cincinnati; Kathryn Kinnucan-Welsch and Patricia Grogan, University of Dayton; Kay Milkie, John Carroll University; Sharon Yates, Ohio University; Belinda Zimmerman, Kent State University; and Jerry Zutell, Ohio State University.

For their courage, commitment, and common sense, we thank our literacy specialists, more than 400 of them at the time of this writing, who openly share their ideas, wonderings, questions, suggestions, and critiques so that we all continue to learn what effective professional development is and what it should be in our professional work.

We acknowledge our LS Project staff members for their dedication and behind-the-scenes support for the project. And, for their diligence and skill in helping us with the manuscript preparation, a special thanks to Deborah Nixon and Therese Longo.

Foreword

Ambitious, comprehensive, statewide, research based, content rich, and implementation focused—not many attempts to improve literacy instruction command these descriptors, but they are appropriate to Ohio's Literacy Specialist (LS) Project, the subject of this book.

Improving early reading instruction commands more attention and resources than most areas of public education. In addition to some widely circulated research reviews, there are thousands of articles and papers available on all facets of reading—how to teach it, assess it, and help those who fall behind. There are dozens of professional development programs competing for attention. The LS Project earned a full share of the spotlight.

This volume by Catherine A. Rosemary, Kathleen A. Roskos, and Leslie K. Landreth represents more than a decade of effort—the work of the authors as well as state education department officials, university faculty, district specialists, teachers, students, and parents. The effort began when the state recognized in the mid-1990s that far too many children could not read by the fourth grade. It continued with the development of a statewide framework that was remarkable for its comprehensiveness and theoretical sophistication. It was the product of extensive stakeholder input, public comment, and numerous drafts and revisions. The resulting framework (presented in Chapter 2) provided both a vision of what Ohio needed to do so that all its students could learn to read and write effectively, and an organizer for the work of planning, developing, implementing, and assessing K–3 literacy education aligned with state standards.

One of the key components of the Ohio framework is ongoing professional development of reading teachers. It is this component and its invention and implementation by the LS Project that is described in detail in this volume.

Buoyed by optimism and hope, the LS Project team determined to rely on theory, evidence, and professional wisdom to invent the literacy specialist system, and on accountability to test and improve it. In the research and development tradition of the Wright Brothers and other Ohio inventors, the LS Project team invented, and built, and tested, and improved a professional development system. They applied to themselves the tools of research and evaluation so that continuous improvement was something they asked not only of teachers, but also of themselves and their colleagues.

Those familiar with education history in the United States know that program implementation is often an orphan left at the schoolhouse door. New policies, programs, standards, books, and materials are often trucked to schools and figuratively dumped on the front steps. Surely, everyone assumes, the teachers and principal will know how to translate expensive, innovative new methods into better learning opportunities for students. Teachers make jokes about the "fad of the year," not because they oppose change, but because they are supremely realistic about how much time and effort it will take to turn theory into sound, consistent practice that improves learning opportunities for students. Just about the time teachers figure out how to work effectively with the now "old" fad, a new one is dropped at the doorstep, and the cycle begins again.

The implementation problem was all too familiar to the LS Project team from their previous experiences rolling out promising programs that never made it into the classroom. They were determined not only that the content they intended that teachers acquire would be of the highest standard, but also that they would hold themselves to a high standard in the design and construction of an implementation system. They began by designing and building a structure drawing on some remarkable resources available throughout the state.

Unless there is a sustaining structure, processes essential to teacher training and development collapse. The LS Project used a network approach to construct a statewide structure. Field faculty (university partners) and literacy specialists (school-based partners) implemented a triadic model of (1) field faculty supporting (2) literacy specialists supporting (3) teachers, in which the former supported the latter, and the latter provided approximately 6 hours a month of training for teachers. Because Ohio has public and private universities located around the state, the LS Project team was able to ground the new structure on an existing one, which was critical to sustaining this ambitious effort. The settings the partners were able to construct and sustain in school sites keyed the success of the LS Project.

A critical, distinguishing feature of the implementation approach was the specification of what the literacy specialists were to do when engaged with participating teachers. To their credit, the LS Project team invented research- and experience-based protocols to guide the specialists. Some object to the idea of protocols in teaching and professional development. Certainly, coaching or consulting of this kind always involves some art. But in the area of literacy instruction and professional development the emergence of consensus protocols are a hallmark of a profession:

> Doctors don't try to figure out a new technique or procedure for every patient who comes to their office, they begin by using standard techniques and procedures that are based on the experience of many doctors over the years. Nobody considers this a way of doctor-proofing medicine, although they have a name for the failure to use standard practices—it's *malpractice*. The standard practices that all doctors (and other professionals) use contain the wisdom of the profession. (Shanker, 1997, p. 36; italics in original)

The LS Project offers a substantial record of protocol use in a statewide comprehensive professional development program and is an impressive demonstration of the benefits of protocols to ensure fidelity of implementation across many coaches and sites.

The triadic structure was deployed in a way that initiated and sustained two critical relationships. First, it fostered ongoing peer collaboration among teachers and among literacy specialists and field faculty. Second, the structure supported leadership that created conditions for professional learning, protected teacher development time, distributed leadership and responsibility, promoted mutual accountability, pressed for and encouraged supportive policies and structures, and integrated activities into a larger comprehensive change process. Without stable settings in which work and learning take place, it is very difficult to move beyond episodic events to sustained programs. Regrettably, times and settings identified at school sites for teachers to learn are often hijacked by other pressing and legitimate concerns and tasks—there is always more to do than time allows, and unfortunately opportunities for teacher learning and development are often lost. The thoughtfulness and foresight that anticipated the value of these relationships is one reason the LS Project warrants the descriptors ambitious, comprehensive, and implementation focused.

"You can't teach what you don't know." This aphorism was sometimes forgotten in the 20th century when infatuation with teaching and learning strategies waxed and concern with content waned. In the last decade, a new evidence base has been developed that readdresses this imbalance. The LS Project team infused all aspects of their program with content knowledge: research, the evidence base for reading, theories of literacy development, pedagogy, English language, and reading and writing strategies, among other content.

In American education professional knowledge for teaching is seldom collected, stored, or shared (Hiebert, Gallimore, & Stigler, 2002). If it is shared, it is in a haphazard manner:

> The successes of [excellent teachers] tend to be born and die with them: beneficial consequences extend only to those pupils who have personal contact with the gifted teachers. No one can measure the waste and loss that have come

from the fact that the contributions of such men and women in the past have been thus confined. (Dewey, 1929, p. 10)

This volume provides a compelling demonstration of what can be achieved when the vision is bold enough and stakeholders take program details seriously. So much public discussion on education and schools is about broad generalities: Who controls the schools? What books, curricula, or standards should be adopted? These are important questions, but in reality they don't matter if no one works on the details. In the classroom, it is the details that matter. In the preparation and development of teachers, they matter. The Ohio LS Project confronted the detail devils and set a worthy example by storing and sharing what they learned.

RONALD GALLIMORE, PhD
Professor Emeritus
University of California, Los Angeles

REFERENCES

Dewey, J. (1929). *The sources of a science of education*. New York: Liveright.
Hiebert, J., Gallimore, R., & Stigler, J. W. (2002). A knowledge base for the teaching profession: What would it look like and how can we get one? *Educational Researcher, 31*(5), 3–15.
Shanker, A. (1997). A national database of lessons. *American Educator, 21*(1/2), 35–36.

Contents

Contents

Introduction

This book is about the Literacy Specialist Project: its development, design, and delivery as a statewide professional development model to improve K–3 reading instruction. In 1999, the Ohio Department of Education initiated the Literacy Specialist Project (hereafter LS Project) with the ambitious aim of improving primary-grade teachers' reading teaching practices. In this book we describe what the LS Project is, what it contains, and how it works. Our intent is twofold: to document the project, now nearly a decade old, and to present it as an example of statewide professional development in primary-grade literacy instruction. The ideas and activities that give meaning and form to the LS Project may be used successfully as they are presented here; they may be modified or adapted to suit the needs of particular states, school districts, buildings, or consortia; and they may be a catalyst for further ideas. Our hope on all counts is that these ideas and activities can be used to inspire and support effective professional development in reading for teachers.

The model of professional development that the LS Project represents is theoretically rooted in Vygotsky's (1978) central thesis that knowledgeable and skillful people can serve as powerful mediators in helping other people to learn and achieve. Tharp and Gallimore (1988) articulated and explained this socio-cultural perspective on human learning as it applies to adults in school settings in their account of the Kamehameha Elementary Education Program (KEEP). Their account, in fact, inspires us and sustains us to this day. Just as a teacher's skillful teaching actions can serve as a scaffold to support a child's progress toward reading and writing competency, a literacy specialist, principal, or other teacher can scaffold other adults' professional learning to promote more skillful

1

practice. Tharp and Gallimore describe the settings in which such professional learning occurs as "contexts of assisted performance," or *activity settings*. In these settings, people intentionally come together in designated places and interact in cultural ways to achieve a shared goal. It is through the network system used in the LS Project that intentional settings are created for colleagues to gather around a common goal of learning new content and skills to improve reading and writing instruction. Thus, grounded in this perspective, the LS Project continues to evolve as a model of professional development.

The design of the LS Project is not simple, as you might expect, given the complexities of professional development to enhance high-quality reading instruction. Toward a simpler rendering of its many facets, we use a pyramidal structure (Figure I.1) as a graphic organizer to visually display key dimensions of the project's professional development model.

Basic tenets form the base of the model and ground its four interlocking faces that describe the model's organization and content. Along with the tenets, the *curriculum and network dimensions* of the model are discussed in the first part of the book. Taking up these dimensions from the start lays out the critical content of the professional development model and its primary delivery system. The midsection of the book focuses on the *activity dimension* of the model, providing a detailed account of how professional development occurs in the LS Project. Readers witness real-life professional development sessions: what they contain, how they are organized, routines and procedures, and what participants say and do. They witness, in other words, the activity that enlivens the model and gives it its unique character and voice. The last part of the book examines the *accountability dimension* of the model, which is ever-present in any statewide effort, and its interface with evaluation, which, in the case of the LS Project model, revolves around a research agenda.

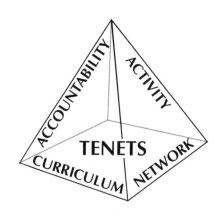

FIGURE I.1. Pyramidal dimensions of the Literacy Specialist Project.

The pyramid graphic provides an advance organizer of what the LS Project is all about and what the professional development model looks like. However, the reader will also benefit from chapter-by-chapter specifics that frame the content of this book.

Chapter 1 discusses the tenets that ground and guide the LS Project. *Tenet* is not a common word, but in this instance, it is the best word because the foundations of the LS Project model are derived from multiple sets of professional development principles (e.g., the Learning First Alliance, 2000). Our tenets are *megaprinciples*, representing an amalgamation of professional opinion.

Moving to the faces of the pyramidal graphic, Chapter 2 describes the structure of the LS Project model, including a state-adopted reading policy framework and a core curriculum for teacher professional learning. The chapter offers an overview of how Ohio conceptualized reading reform and describes its "conceptual framework." The framework is state-specific, but it is quite clear that it contains elements commonly found in standards-based reform efforts geared to improvements in students' reading achievement across the United States in the last decade. The critical role of professional development in meeting reform goals is highlighted and carried forward in a description of the core curriculum—the heart of the LS Project. The chapter provides a detailed description of the core curriculum and its interrelated learning domains of knowing, planning, teaching, and assessing. Types of knowledge and cognitive processes that the core curriculum affords educators as learners are identified. The chapter closes with a brief description of the 15 professional development sessions that represent the scope and sequence of the curriculum.

The central focus of Chapter 3 is the LS Project's delivery system, which uses a network approach. How to mobilize and organize people for large-scale delivery of professional development is one of the most challenging problems in "scaling up" a model. This chapter introduces key players who implement professional development statewide, specifically field faculty (university-based partners) and literacy specialists (school-based partners). How the LS Project marshaled these human resources to meet the need for widespread professional development is instructive for program planning in both large- and small-scale professional development designs.

Chapter 4 shifts to the dimension of activity, taking readers into the "life" of the network system. First, readers enter the literacy specialists' network where a field faculty member is preparing her literacy specialist group for a professional development session with classroom teachers in their local schools. Readers then follow a literacy specialist from this preparatory session into her own delivery of a session with a group of classroom teachers in her own school district. These close-up views help readers to grasp how the professional development model works at different levels—from field faculty to literacy specialist to teacher—for purposes of implementing the core curriculum in school-based sessions.

The next two chapters follow classroom teachers from their participation in a professional development session into their own classrooms where they practice new principles, procedures, and higher-order teaching skills (e.g., scaffolding). Chapter 5 describes two kinds of professional development extensions that attempt to situate teacher learning in practice: *Field Work* and a segment referred to as *Making Connections*. The value-added of authentic *Field Work* is highlighted. *Field Work* involves teachers in practicing new instructional procedures, gathering student work samples, and preparing for the next session in providing effective professional development. In Chapter 6, readers can observe coaching in action, which is probably the most intimate and complex professional learning activity. We also feature the Teacher Learning Instrument (the TLI), a metacognitive tool for assisting teaching skill to higher levels of instructional performance. In the LS Project model, this tool is used to guide coaching activity and to create conditions for collaborative inquiry.

The final chapters of the book address the fourth face of the pyramid: matters of accountability and research in professional development programs. Chapter 7 is devoted to a discussion of the what, how, and to whom the LS Project as a professional development model must give account as one of its primary responsibilities. The methodologies and tools used to develop, monitor, evaluate, and inform the five pyramidal dimensions of the LS Project model are presented and illustrated. Practical matters of management, resource allocation, and reporting to multiple audiences are also discussed. Chapter 8 describes the project's research agenda for examining the model's impact on teacher knowledge and classroom practice. Although still in its early stages, the research evidence shows that the LS Project is making progress toward the goal of ongoing professional development that supports improvements in students' academic reading achievement. The final section of the chapter takes a look ahead to the research the LS Project still needs to do if it is to contribute to the evidence base on high-quality professional development in literacy education.

Before turning to a full account of the LS Project model, we offer a few more introductory thoughts. We imagine that you, our readers, will be a diverse group of individuals interested in improving students' literacy achievement. Professional developers, state department program directors, and school administrators may find our book helpful as they consider the design of large-scale professional learning programs to improve reading instruction. Literacy coaches (e.g., in Title I) and teacher educators may find it useful for planning and delivering professional development sessions in district and/or school settings to enhance teachers' knowledge and skills for effective literacy teaching. University instructors can use this book as a resource in their administrator preparation courses in leadership and professional development. And our colleagues engaged in similar efforts may find some points of comparison and insights that inform their unique professional development approaches and programs.

Now for a few words about us: We are teacher–educators who serve the university world, schools, and state government. Each of us teaches university courses in reading methods. Each has directed or assisted in directing the LS Project under state auspices at different times. Each has published or has contributed in other ways to research related to the project.

With colleagues in higher education, state leaders, school administrators, and teachers, we conceptualized the LS Project. With them, we labored to write the core curriculum and to repeatedly revise it. We helped one another recruit literacy specialists in school districts and together supported them in their first efforts to teach their peers. We persevered with our colleagues despite time constraints, interruptions, and apathy. Together we have lobbied and argued loudly for state funding, and pursued joint goals for teacher professional development. While we each led in moving the LS Project forward, we also often followed the lead of literacy specialists who provided feedback from the field, state leaders who pointed the project in new directions, and higher education faculty who argued vigorously for specific topics and content revisions. So, while we may author the account of the LS Project as a professional development model, we did not compose its meaning and content by ourselves. It is a model created and sustained by many dedicated educators who are committed to the best literacy education for all students.

All this said, there are some special features about the book worth noting as you read. Each chapter opens with an excerpt from, and many chapters other excerpts from, the project's newsletter: *The LS Exchange*. We hope these pieces will let you hear the voices of many of those who contributed to the evolution of the LS Project and the professional learning gained through their collaboration. We include many figures and appendices (e.g., data collection forms, full-blown professional development session descriptions, letters, memorandums, matrices to help readers). We hope readers will use these tangible tools-of-the-trade that helped us keep track of people, activities, and outcomes as we continued to grow and sustain the LS Project. What matters most to us, though, is that you, our readers, find what we have to report informative, educative, and above all practical in realizing your own professional development goals—large and small.

CHAPTER 1

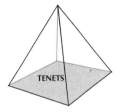

Tenets

Tenet 1:	**Tenet 2:**	**Tenet 3:**
Professional Development Expands and Deepens Knowledge	Professional Development Creates Favorable Conditions for Learning	Professional Development Builds Relationships

At the heart of effective literacy instruction is the knowledgeable teacher who understands the foundations of literacy and skillfully applies proven strategies.

—*The LS Exchange* (Vol. 1, p. 4, 2000)

As we write this book, professional development is very much in the spotlight, increasingly seen as a powerful means for improving student achievement and learning. The assumption that professional practice improves when practitioners continue to learn is not new. Indeed, it is a strongly held belief in most professions, including medicine, architecture, and law. Professional development as a matter of course in teaching practice, however, is a relatively new idea, one that emerged only in the latter part of the 20th century (Roskos & Vukelich, 1998; Sykes, 1999). Before that time, teachers experienced few job-embedded learning opportunities for professional learning. Instead, they relied heavily on professional organizations as sources of new learning outside of higher education coursework. But today, both professional educational organizations and federal and state legislative bodies view professional development as essential to education reform and are more invested in assuring that teachers have an ongoing opportunity to learn as an integral part of their practice. The No Child Left

Behind Act of 2001, for example, requires annual reporting by states of teachers' participation in high-quality professional development as defined in the law (U.S. Department of Education, 2001).

With the growing recognition (and expectation) of teachers as learners who benefit from ongoing professional development comes a new responsibility for ensuring that professional development is high quality and leads to higher levels of teaching performance. We note common themes, principles, understandings, and elements that constitute effective professional development. Syntheses of research on professional development describe the knowledge base for making decisions about effective professional development programs (e.g., Hawley, 2005; Hawley & Valli, 1999). Based on this evidence, various professional organizations, federal and state government programs, and think tanks have taken steps to guide the design of high-quality professional development that supports professional learning. *Every Child Reading: A Professional Development Guide,* published by the Learning First Alliance (2000), for example, puts forward guidelines for the content, context, and methodology of professional development in reading instruction, based on the best available research. Other professional groups offer guidelines that serve as strong standards for the structure, content, and delivery of high-quality professional development (see, e.g., National Partnership for Excellence and Accountability in Teaching, 2001).

From studying different sets of guidelines, examining the research on professional development, considering the testimony of professional developers, and taking into account our own professional development experience, we have distilled three tenets of professional development that serve as the foundation of the LS Project. Stronger than pieces of advice, the tenets are a set of articles to which we are firmly committed if the professional development model in the LS Project is to progress from good to great in the sense of high quality (Collins, 2001). Anything that does not fit with the tenets we will not do because it distracts from a simple, crystalline understanding of what the LS Project is and can potentially become. For example, a workshop approach to professional development would not suffice in the LS Project. High-quality professional development must expand and deepen content and pedagogical knowledge, must allow ample time for collaborative problem solving in the professional development setting, must require teachers to apply new knowledge to practice, and must build relationships that will support a learning community.

TENET 1: PROFESSIONAL DEVELOPMENT EXPANDS AND DEEPENS KNOWLEDGE

The old saying "You can't teach what you don't know" holds true when it comes to literacy pedagogy. Knowledge is at the very core of the kind of effective professional development that leads to effective reading and writing instruction in the elementary school. Teachers need to know what they are doing if they are to be masterful, deliberate, strategic, and sensitive in their literacy practice.

But what is meant by "knowledge"? In the most basic sense, *knowledge* refers to the content or substance of a given subject matter—in our case, the subject matter is literacy pedagogy, and most specifically reading education in the primary grades. In our professional community, the body of knowledge (i.e., the content)—or what teachers should know and be able to do—is defined by the International Reading Association (2004a), which establishes standards about the knowledge, skills, and dispositions of candidates when they complete a particular level of preparation. (See *Standards for Reading Professionals* in Figure 1.1.)

The International Reading Association standards embody what some have termed the "historically shared knowledge" of the content domain arrived at through consensus by scholars, researchers, and teachers in the literacy field (Anderson & Krathwohl, 2001, p. 13). Professional development, therefore, should be grounded in the International Reading Association standards to ensure that teachers are acquiring the body of knowledge they need to become expert in their practice. Such grounding also shows that the professional development content is research based because it reflects the "historically shared

---

1 **Foundational Knowledge:** Candidates have knowledge of the foundations of reading and writing processes and instruction.

2 **Instructional Strategies and Curriculum Materials:** Candidates use a wide range of instructional practices, approaches, methods, and curriculum materials to support reading and writing instruction.

3 **Assessment, Diagnosis, and Evaluation:** Candidates use a variety of assessment tools and practices to plan and evaluate effective reading instruction.

4 **Creating a Literate Environment:** Candidates create a literate environment that fosters reading and writing by integrating foundational knowledge, use of instructional practices, approaches and methods, curriculum materials, and the appropriate use of assessments.

5 **Professional Development:** Candidates view professional development as a careerlong effort and responsibility.

FIGURE 1.1. The International Reading Association's (2004a) *Standards for Reading Professionals: Revised 2003.*

knowledge" of the content domain, including the scientific research base. In the professional development provided through the LS Project, for example, teachers extend their knowledge of literacy development, the English language, teaching strategies in essential components of reading and writing instruction, and assessment tools and processes.

In the design of professional development, however, two points about knowledge should be kept very much in mind. One is that knowledge is not static. What teachers need to know and need to be able to do for effective reading instruction *changes* as new ideas and evidence are accepted by the professional community. Consider, for example, how much new research regarding children's language and literacy development before school entry has affected preschool and kindergarten language arts curricula. Best practice, as defined by the field, includes essentials of early literacy instruction, such as oral language, comprehension, phonological awareness activities, alphabet activities, support for emergent reading and writing, and integrated, content-focused activities in preschool and kindergarten educational settings (Dickinson & Neuman, 2005; International Reading Association and the National Association for the Education of Young Children, 1998; Roskos, Christie, & Richgels, 2003). Thus, the changing, evolving nature of knowledge must be taken into account in professional development and steps must be taken to cultivate scientific thinking in its approach (Stanovich & Stanovich, 2003).

The other point is that knowledge should not be confused with the materials used to package it, such as textbooks, courses, curriculum products, and, increasingly, online courses. Instructional materials select, sort, and store knowledge, but they do not constitute it. Materials, in other words, facilitate the presentation of knowledge (i.e., the what and the how of the discipline), which reaches beyond the often narrow boundaries of material resources. Professional development, then, cannot be limited to a package: a textbook, a presentation, a course. Rather, it must focus on developing the educator's knowledge of the subject-matter domain (i.e., reading pedagogy), where materials serve as the means, not as the ends.

Two key points about knowledge as defined in the LS Project:

- Knowledge is not static.
- Instructional materials select, sort, and store knowledge, but they do not constitute it.

It is fair to say that, from the start, the university faculty, expert teachers, and state leaders who shaped the LS Project struggled considerably with the matter of knowledge and still do for several reasons—some more philosophical than others. At the start of the LS Project, we had to answer two questions with some specificity. Our first question was *What should primary-grade teachers know and be able to do to achieve effective reading instruction for all students?*

Answering this question meant achieving a consensus about the content of the professional development in the project, which we did as laid out in the core curriculum described in the next chapter. But a real workable consensus was not easy to achieve. It meant asking hard questions and confronting brutal truths about what is essential for teachers to learn and what ideas fall into such categories as fads, fancies, and favorites. It meant taking substantial time to engage in dialogue and debate without getting defensive and without placing blame. It meant creating a culture wherein everyone at the table had a tremendous opportunity to be heard and ultimately for shared meanings to be forged.

Put into place at the onset of the LS Project (and strategies still used today), this process for achieving consensus led to the hard-won, deeply felt aim of the LS Project, namely, to develop teachers' *understanding* of literacy pedagogy, defined as "the ability to think and act flexibly with what one knows" (Perkins, 1998, p. 40). Understanding is evident when educators can *explain* effective reading instruction by providing comprehensive, scientifically supported, and justifiable accounts of their practice; when they can *interpret* literacy education ideas to others with clarity, logic, and accuracy; when they can *apply* scientifically based evidence in everyday instruction; and when they can *reflect*, by showing a willingness to critique their own practice and to consider multiple perspectives on literacy education. These abilities—the markers of deep understanding—safeguard practice from what Dewey (1933) referred to as the "tyranny of technique," where blind adherence to procedures can ignore classroom realities. On this point turned a second major question in the LS Project design: *Should professional development open with theory or with practice?*

Some were adamant that professional development should begin with a review of basic knowledge and theory, such as models of literacy development. There is nothing so practical as a good theory, they argued, and a good grasp of theoretical concepts can liberate teachers' instructional decision making. Others openly challenged the theory-to-practice order of things in professional development. They retorted: Don't practicing teachers know all this already from their prior educational experiences? Isn't this mimicking the traditional college course, which too often dwells on theory at the expense of practical instructional sequences and strategies necessary for effective literacy instruction? Why not start with more practical (and pressing) matters, such as reading assessment? Wouldn't practical areas of everyday teaching (e.g., teaching techniques) be more inviting to teachers, who are motivated to improve their extant practice?

The questions sparked spirited debate, and ended in consensus that competence alone will not produce great results. Many a competent teacher has proceeded with accuracy and precision oblivious to everyday practices incongruent with his or her students' needs. No, the important goal of professional development is to engage teachers in very rigorous thinking with complex ideas, *then* to take *disciplined action* within a framework of evidence-based literacy education. So it was agreed that for top-notch reading instruction, teachers must *first* be knowledgeable about the scientific roots of effective practices and critical consumers of research, and *then* be competent practitioners. The knowledge base, we agreed, could be captured in four major components of literacy content: literacy development, English language, reading and writing processes, and models and methods of reading and writing instruction. Drawing on this knowledge base, teachers then extend and apply knowledge in the pedagogical domains of planning, teaching, and assessing. These four domains—knowing, planning, teaching, and assessing—constitute the curricular framework of the professional development in the LS Project; they are fully explicated in Chapter 2. In sum, our stance is that professional development must begin and end with a knowledge emphasis—in acquiring the known, in critiquing the known, and in generating the new.

TENET 2: PROFESSIONAL DEVELOPMENT CREATES FAVORABLE CONDITIONS FOR LEARNING

Assuming that knowledge is the core of excellent teaching practice, we then grappled with the question *How do teachers learn the knowledge they need to continuously improve their practice?*

Presently, adult learning theory and research offer several insights on this matter. We know, for example, that adulthood includes at least three developmental turning points: intimacy versus isolation in early adulthood; generativity versus stagnation in middle adulthood; and integrity versus despair in old age (Erikson, 1985). We also know that these transitions can influence professional life (Sprinthall, Reiman, & Thies-Sprinthall, 1996). We know that adults' reflective judgment abilities appear to increase in complexity with experience, thus improving their capability to learn from experience (King & Kitchener, 2004). Experience, in turn, is the adult's most valued resource when engaging in new learning situations, and what adults rely (and overrely) on to grasp new ideas (Brookfield, 1986). We know that adults pass through different career phases across their professional lives, characterized broadly as survival to competency building to a period of stability (Burden & Byrd, 1990). Thus, interplay of adults' development and learning as they age has implications for the design and implementation of professional development activities. Young adults just beginning their teaching career have different needs, for example, than career changers who are older with more extensive life experiences.

Certainly adults learn differently from children—but perhaps not all that differently. From a "new science of learning" perspective (Bransford, Brown, & Cocking, 2000; Rose & Meyer, 2002), adult learning is like all human learning. It happens best when:

- The emphasis is on learning with understanding over the rote memorization of facts and the reproduction of knowledge;
- Preexisting knowledge serves as the basis for new learning; and
- Learning is active, motivating learners' attention, engaging them in combining and constructing knowledge, and providing many opportunities to practice emerging skills.

Underneath it all are neural networks that all human beings possess and that drive them to seek patterns in information, to search for desirable strategies in order to organize information, and to use emotion for maintaining engagement with new information (Zull, 2002).

While these universals do not provide us with the specifics of how adults learn, they do identify the basic elements needed to create favorable conditions for professional learning. In many respects, we might consider these the nonnegotiables that must be part and parcel of professional development design. In the LS Project, these are (1) identifying the knowledge to be learned for effective reading instruction, including pedagogical content knowledge (i.e., ways to represent and formulate reading content); (2) acknowledging and building on teachers' practical experience; (3) involving teachers in planning for and monitoring their own professional learning; and (4) providing a supportive learning environment to meet individual needs.

To embed these universals in professional development, the LS Project sets high standards for the learning environment. It requires a monthly 3-hour block of time before, during, or after school for instruction with extensive classroom-based fieldwork in between professional development sessions. It focuses on the "materials of practice" (Ball & Cohen, 1999), such as student work, reporting forms (e.g., report cards), and instructional resources (e.g., teaching materials) as key sources of new learning and instructional problem solving. Professional books, articles, and media are used to extend teachers' understanding of concepts, with an emphasis on higher-order pedagogical reasoning skills, such as inductive reasoning and critical and creative thinking. It calls for small-group collaborative problem solving that follows an iterative process of asking questions, engaging in dialogue and debate, confronting realities, and making evidence-based judgments. It meets teachers' needs but only as these align with students' needs to achieve state benchmarks in reading. The professional development press is not just about teachers' instructional actions, but about their engaging in disciplined thought, *followed by* deliberate action. Features of the

professional learning environment combine to complement the larger comprehensive change process of school and district in the spirit of continuous
improvement (Costa & Kallick, 1995).

Favorable conditions for professional learning in the LS Project
include:

- Ample time devoted to learning and applying.
- Focus on "materials of practice."
- Emphasis on critical thinking skills.
- Problem solving in small groups.
- Teachers' needs are aligned with students' needs.
- Disciplined thought followed by deliberate action.
- Engagement in continuous improvement process.

Creating learning environments of this caliber encountered unavoidable
and, some might argue, predictable problems in the LS Project, although we did
not necessarily foresee them (Trubowitz, 2000). Time, space, and laser-focused
activity are precious commodities in schools as in all organizations. Unions have
established rules that can affect job roles, assignment changes, meeting times,
and locations. Leadership can shift, change, come, and go. Getting the project
off the ground in some school districts was not without its challenges. In some
cases, we needed to meet face-to-face with administrators and union representa-
tives to explain the project goals and activities and to discuss how these could fit
within their school structure and improvement plans. This extra time and effort
usually resulted in the district choosing to participate in the project and helped
us to better understand local conditions and constraints to implementing the
project.

Collaboration between teachers and between professional development
goals and those of the school may not be part of the teaching culture. Thus, considerable energy must go toward learning collaboration skills and accepting new
roles in the environment. Administrative pressure for quick results in teachers'
practice evidenced in students' reading achievement is inevitable, even though
completely unrealistic given the strong resistance to change in teachers' practice
and the longitudinal results necessary to make claims about change in students'
performance.

Still, in most school settings, those involved in the LS Project created productive learning environments that afforded time and opportunity for teachers
to learn and develop a sense of community, camaraderie, and even joy in
learning together. Beyond this, they helped to build an enduring culture of
learning—full of knowledgeable teachers who take responsibility for improving
their own practice.

TENET 3: PROFESSIONAL DEVELOPMENT
BUILDS RELATIONSHIPS

One of the more satisfying aspects of teaching is knowing that once you close the classroom door, you are in charge. It is true that what should be done in the classroom is described, explained, demanded, probed, and prescribed from many different quarters. But in the end it is the teacher who actually decides what will happen and how activities will go once the door closes. That sense of autonomy can be exhilarating.

This historic benefit of teaching, however, is also one of its biggest drawbacks because it can lead to working in isolation, and this, in the end, stalls learning. When teachers become isolated from their peers and the professional community, they become intellectually secluded as well and grow to overrely on their everyday experience and gut reactions in making instructional decisions. As a result, their practice runs a higher risk of error, because there is little objective feedback to reveal faulty thinking, inaccurate implementation of techniques, and misinterpretations of information. Thus encapsulated, the teachers' practice grows ever more resistant to new knowledge from sources other than personal experience. And so it is that outmoded techniques and methods, refuted by research, persist long after they should have been abandoned in favor of more robust approaches. The teacher's practice becomes closed to critical examination and fails to transcend intuition and common sense. It becomes, in short, unreflective, lacking in the scientific thinking necessary for informed and reflective practice (Fishman & McCarthy, 1998; McAninch, 1993).

To ensure reflective practice, professional development must develop reflective teachers—"those who inquire into their own practice and who examine their own classrooms to find out what works best" (Stanovich & Stanovich, 2003, p. 4). For this to happen, professional development must build relationships among educators.

At least two relationship-building strategies are critical. One is ongoing collaboration among teams of educators who meet regularly to plan together, to learn together, and to critically examine their work together. The other is skillful leadership that creates conditions for professional learning (e.g., time), distributes leader responsibility and accountability, establishes supportive policies and organizational structures, and integrates activities into a larger comprehensive change process aimed at continuous improvement of teaching and learning literacy in schools (Corcoran & Goertz, 1995).

Living the tenet of building relationships is the most invigorating and, when all is said and done, perhaps the most rewarding for everyone involved in the LS Project. Human relationships are the social glue of the LS Project and enliven it with purpose, emotion, and meaning. They help inspire individual motivation to learn and instill commitment to the work, especially when it is at its most challenging. For this very human reason, the LS Project uses a relational organizational structure that connects state agency personnel, university faculty, school-based literacy specialists, and classroom teachers in a learning network.

Several strategies helped to build and strengthen the human ties that hold the LS Project together. Less tangible than some, but absolutely critical is a clarity of purpose that is well known by all. This is often referred to as "the vision" or what should become the reality in the sphere of action. In our case, *the vision or aim is teachers' sound understanding of literacy pedagogy so as to practice high-quality literacy instruction that serves the common good.*

It is not enough to have a vision, though. That is not the determining strategy. Rather, the powerful strategy is to heed the vision in all aspects of project activities so as not to lose sight of it in the everyday work of getting the job done. It is the persistent, dogged attention to it that realizes the vision. This demands extreme diligence and constancy of purpose. It means saying "no" to some glittering opportunities, and making "stop-doing" lists just as often as "to-do" lists so as to maintain focus on what the LS Project is deeply committed to: developing teachers' understanding of literacy pedagogy. In our project, the design and implementation of the core curriculum (described in Chapter 2) helped us to use the vision-oriented strategy effectively because it kept us focused on the larger aim of developing teacher understanding while immersed in the detail of making it happen in schools and classrooms.

We employed another effective strategy to build relationships: small-group learning. Different professional development projects have used the small-group strategy with considerable success, such as the National Writing Project (Firestone & Pennell, 1997) and the Book Club Connection (McMahon, Raphael, Goatley, & Pardo, 1997). In our project, we used the strategy in multiple ways: (1) to form the field faculty network, which brought together reading faculty from different higher education institutions and state department of education leaders; (2) to prepare literacy specialists for their professional developer role in collaboration with field faculty; (3) to structure the professional development at the school level where literacy specialists worked with small groups of about 15 teachers; and (4) to engage teachers with the content during professional development sessions. Engaged in accomplishing the professional development goals of the project, the small groups became closely knit social networks that each discussed its unique needs and problems, but also exchanged more global ideas with one another that affected them all as partners and collaborators in the project. The big advantage of the small-group strategy was its flexibility to meet local goals and needs, yet preserve the larger purpose of the professional development from a statewide perspective.

We also used the familiar strategy of gathering everyone together at a conference to kick off the year and to end it in celebration of what had been accomplished. We made sure these 2-day events had plenty of opportunities for whole-group learning where cutting-edge ideas were introduced and explored, for example, exemplary professional development for quality literacy instruction in schools (Hoffman, 2001), data-based decision making for educators (Clay, 2002), social context of teaching and learning (Gallimore, 2003), biology of learning (Zull, 2004), principles of professional development (Hawley, 2005), and a schoolwide change model (Goldenberg, 2006).

Relationship-building strategies in the LS Project:

- Ongoing collaboration among teams of educators who meet together regularly to plan, learn, and critically examine their work.
- Skillful leadership that creates conditions for professional learning, distributes leader responsibility and accountability, establishes supportive policies and organizational structures, and integrates activities into a larger comprehensive change process aimed at continuous improvement of teaching and learning literacy in schools.
- Shared goal of developing teachers' understanding of literacy pedagogy to improve teaching skill.
- Commitment to and maintaining focus on the shared goal.
- Small-group learning to meet local needs yet preserve the larger purpose of the professional development from a statewide perspective.
- Large conferences where cutting-edge ideas are introduced and explored for whole-group learning.

Conference schedules allowed ample time for participants to assemble and reassemble into small groups for problem solving on curricular issues related to professional development, for conversations on coaching, and for sharing local initiatives. We also included plenty of time during the conferences for social talk before whole- and small-group sessions, between them, and after them, so the participants in the project could exchange ideas informally, build friendships, and enjoy one another's company. When the content of a conference is meaningful and intellectually stimulating, the value of this time for social interaction is invaluable. It taps the social oil that fuels positive affect for an endeavor or challenging work, which, in turn, leads to deep engagement with the work and interest in the content. Needless to say, we soon recognized and tapped the potential of social talk and playfulness for making a difference in the project's progress toward its ambitious aim.

CLOSING

Different educational organizations have proposed research-based principles of professional development in an effort to steer more rigorous professional learning (e.g., National Staff Development Council, Learning First Alliance). States too are creating frameworks for high-quality professional development as a critical component of standards-based education in order to meet the requirements of the No Child Left Behind Act of 2001. New strategies for implementing effective professional development in alignment with research-based principles are also being proposed and tested in professional development contexts (e.g., Robelen, 2003).

We are alert to these initiatives as they help us gauge the strength and sustainability of our guiding tenets. Evidence of such links is a good indicator that our guiding principles are solid. Consequently, we can have more confidence in the decisions we have made and continue to make in upholding these tenets as we continue to lead and coordinate the project. Our ways of upholding these tenets also has grown more varied and stronger in producing desired outcomes. As the project has grown over the past 6 years, we have added university reading faculty and expanded the project's reach to more schools. Given its dynamic nature, the project has adapted to increasing demands for accountability. Examples of accountability are presented in Chapter 7. Today these tenets serve the project well as foundational assumptions. Altogether, we have developed a much fuller appreciation of how a small set of beliefs can help steer a large-scale project.

Our account of the LS Project continues in the next chapter with a description of the state's reading policy framework and the core curriculum—a centerpiece of the professional development in its structure, content, and processes.

CHAPTER 2

Foundations

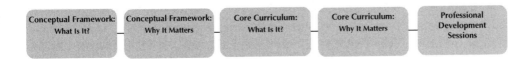

| Conceptual Framework: What Is It? | Conceptual Framework: Why It Matters | Core Curriculum: What Is It? | Core Curriculum: Why It Matters | Professional Development Sessions |

> The core curriculum, organized around a set of understandings, creates a shared understanding among educators that links research and practice. It also lays the foundations for standards of practice that help create an equitable educational process for all children.
>
> —*The LS Exchange* (Vol. 1, p. 4, 2000)

In this chapter, we explain two prime drivers of the LS Project, a conceptual framework of state-level reading policy and a core curriculum of statewide professional development in primary-grade reading and writing instruction. Readers will find this information useful because it further establishes the project's setting and provides background knowledge about its professional development activities. We explain why the project is structured the way it is and detail specifics about the content of the professional development, which centers on a core curriculum. We also show in the description that follows how these two sets of ideas serve to guide and stabilize the project, and thus move us closer to the ideal of continuous, ongoing professional development of the primary-grade teacher's literacy practice.

CONCEPTUAL FRAMEWORK: WHAT IS IT?

For 2 consecutive years, 1996–1998, Ohio's reading performance had declined and no group had met the state's 75% benchmark on the reading test. Something had to be done to improve students' chances for reading success. In response to mounting concerns about the reading performance of fourth graders on state proficiency tests and a growing reading achievement gap between highest- and lowest-performing student groups in the state, the Ohio Department of Education launched a comprehensive state policy targeting educational reform in a standards-based context.

As envisioned, the LS Project is one element of the comprehensive state policy targeting educational reform in a standards-based context. It was not, therefore, conceived as a magic bullet for wide-scale reading improvement. Rather, it was intended to work conjointly with other initiatives to meet the goal of improving students' reading achievement. Formulated by Ohio's Department of Education (1999), the conceptual framework envisions a statewide literacy initiative. Its basic ideas are not that different from those found in other states' literacy initiatives that emerged in the last decades of the 20th century. The basic elements of the framework emphasize collaborative relationships between ideas, events, programs, activities, and processes that build capacity for entire communities to ensure that all students become successful readers. The graphic in Figure 2.1 depicts the Ohio Literacy Conceptual Framework during the formative years of the LS Project.

Let's look closely at the structure of the graphic itself. As we do, be mindful that the concepts apply to a state's entire P–12 system of literacy education. Thus these ideas are large in scope, meant to encompass the many varieties and particularities of specific districts and schools.

The concentric circles in the figure (state, district, building, and classroom) represent the multiple environments that both shape and respond to the literacy development and achievement of individuals. Essentially, this is an ecological view of how things work based on a well-established scientific theory of human development. Each of us is the product of an ongoing interaction between the influence of our personal life experiences and the contribution of our unique genetic endowment within the culture in which we live (Bransford et al., 2000; Bronfenbrenner, 1994, 1995; Bronfenbrenner & Morris, 1998; Shonkoff & Phillips, 2004). At the very core of this view is the home where children first encounter the literacy practices of their family, kin, and friends, and which they bring with them into their educational experiences in early care and educational settings and into school. As reading educators, we recognize both the complexities and the power of these environments for influencing students' literacy achievement. The now classic study by Betty Hart and Todd Risley (Hart, 2000; Hart & Risley, 1995), for example, shows how language use in the home carries forward

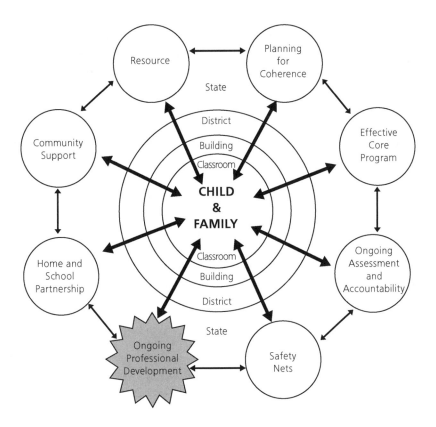

FIGURE 2.1. Ohio Literacy Initiative Conceptual Framework.

to reading achievement in school. As their data show, a 3-year-old's vocabulary is a strong predictor of reading comprehension in third grade.

The small circles represent components that districts and schools should consider in planning and implementing literacy initiatives, programs, instruction, and assessments to help students achieve literacy standards. Note that *ongoing professional development* is one among eight components that can be combined (and recombined) with the others to create optimal conditions for students' literacy learning in school.

The continuous arrows between the components show their interconnectedness. A school, for example, follows an assessment and accountability plan that includes safety nets in the form of interventions to prevent reading failure, as well as professional development for administrators and teachers to effectively deploy them. Thus, the components of the framework operate in concert to gain power to achieve the goal of reading mastery for all students. From a systems theory perspective, this reflects the basic premise that the whole is greater than the sum of its parts. Working together, the components are stronger and likely to have more impact than when each works alone.

The bold arrows that radiate across the graphic symbolize the pathways that should encourage communication and relationship building between environments and components of a strong system of literacy education. As defined in systems theory, a *system* is a "network of relationships"—an integrated whole, the properties of which cannot be reduced to those of its smaller parts (Capra, 1996, p. 37). Although the conceptual framework may go through revision to keep current with scientifically based reading research and changes in federal and state policy (e.g., new ideas and requirements of the No Child Left Behind Act), the framework reflects systems thinking, acknowledging the dynamic nature of literacy teaching and learning in states, districts, schools, classrooms, and homes. It appreciates that individual literacy achievement results from a "dynamic web of interrelated events" (Capra, 1996, p. 39).

Recognizing that teaching quality does make a difference in students' achievement, state leaders increasingly viewed large-scale professional development as a viable means of changing the odds for children. They took action, launching the LS Project as a promising large-scale professional development framework for K–3 classroom teachers.

CONCEPTUAL FRAMEWORK: WHY IT MATTERS

These days, educators are only too familiar with frameworks, models, blueprints, systems, and accountability plans. Through widely disseminated research syntheses (e.g., Adams, 1990; National Reading Panel, 2000; Snow, Burns, & Griffin, 1998; Snow, Griffin, & Burns, 2005), the reading profession has the benefit of a strong and growing scientific research base, which at the same time makes it a more complex professional discipline and therefore more demanding of educator professional skills and insights. The more we know about reading and writing processes and effective teaching strategies that boost student learning, the greater the demand for knowledgeable and skillful teachers who can make a positive impact on student achievement. Looking at the conceptual framework as a state-level literacy initiative, we know that a lot of energy went into its development, from intense discussion with stakeholder groups, to reading and responding to thousands of e-mails about it, to numerous revisions and rough drafts, to the final plans for dissemination, not to mention the many informative workshops held to explain it. In this respect, the framework holds considerable intellectual capital. So why does this matter? We have two short answers to this question.

The first is that the conceptual framework provides a vision of what must be done for all students to read, write, and participate effectively in the world. Lacking a vision, educators can get things done and still make little or no progress. A vision creates a worthy end-in-view that everyone can see and rally around, a view that focuses our collective attention on attaining larger goals beyond local, individual concerns, one that provides us with "terminals of deliberation" for considering the present and anticipating possibilities for the future to enlarge the common good (Dewey, 1964). The important benefit of a vision is direction toward a higher purpose. To its advantage, the LS Project is a part of the vision that the conceptual framework seeks to illuminate.

Our second short answer is that the conceptual framework offers an organizer for accomplishing the work of planning, developing, implementing, and assessing K–3 literacy education at the local level in sync with state English language arts academic content standards and literacy goals. How to get started with a comprehensive change process at the building or district level is a daunting task. In addition to mobilizing others to action, there are so many things to consider: curriculum, instruction, assessment, community relations, and interventions. Sorting information and breaking down activity into manageable chunks for teams to do can become a real challenge. The conceptual framework helps local leadership to meet this challenge by offering a guide to action that is flexible and adaptable to local conditions, such as timing, resources, current initiatives, and mandates. At the same time, it can serve as an arbiter when challenged with making hard-edged decisions about what to do and when in order to achieve literacy goals responsibly and in a timely manner. These functions of the conceptual framework put the LS Project at an advantage by embedding it in the organizational work of systemic and systematic change efforts at the local level.

CORE CURRICULUM: WHAT IS IT?

The LS Project is founded on a research-based core curriculum for educators, *Teaching Reading and Writing: A Core Curriculum for Educators* (Roskos, 2000). The core curriculum identifies foundational knowledge, skills, and dispositions that classroom teachers need for effective instructional practice based on research and professional organization standards (American Federation of Teachers, 1995; Ball & Cohen, 1999; Hawley & Valli, 1999; International Reading Association, 2004a; International Reading Association and the National Association for the Education of Young Children, 1998; Learning First Alliance, 2000; National Reading Panel, 2000; Snow et al., 1998). The curriculum links research and practice and serves to create a shared knowledge base among teachers. It sets standards of teaching practice that promote equitable literacy education for all students.

In the simplest terms, the core curriculum is a document that university faculty, expert teachers, and state leaders agreed would be the centerpiece of the professional development in the LS Project. It identifies essential knowledge and processes in literary pedagogy consistent with the current professional knowledge base (e.g., International Reading Association, 2004a; National Early Literacy Panel [see Strickland & Shanahan, 2004]; National Reading Panel, 2000; National Research Council, 2000). It is represented in a four-section, three-column table that we label the *core curriculum matrix* (Figure 2.2). The sections and columns of the table contain the learning domains, curricular components, and conceptual elements that identify essential knowledge and cognitive processes of effective literacy teaching. These parts of the curriculum framework are explained in the next sections under the subheadings Learning Domains, Curriculum Components, and Conceptual Elements.

The core curriculum is one way to organize the staggering amount of content on the teaching of beginning reading and writing. It offers a viable framework for defining expectations and learning objectives, assessing the quality of the professional development experience, and investigating the impact of professional development content on teacher learning and student literacy achievement. It serves as the curriculum scope and sequence for the professional development that literacy specialists offer to teachers in schools.

Learning Domains

The core curriculum is organized into four domains of teaching practice—knowing, planning, teaching, and assessing—common to pedagogical frameworks (e.g., Danielson, 1996) and professional standards (e.g., International Reading Association, 2004a; National Council for Accreditation of Teacher Education, 2004). These domains can be thought of as large categories or "bins" that contain the curricular content to be learned in the teaching of beginning reading and writing.

The knowing domain focuses on what teachers should know in order to make professional decisions about reading and writing instruction. More specifically, it addresses four knowledge categories (Krathwohl, 2002) in the discipline of literacy pedagogy: factual knowledge, conceptual knowledge, procedural knowledge, and metacognitive knowledge.

The factual knowledge category contains the basic elements teachers must know if they are to practice the discipline and solve problems in it. For example, they need to know the terminology used in the teaching of reading and writing. Terms such as *alphabetic principle*, *segmenting*, *developmental spelling*, and *primer* have special meanings in the teaching of reading and writing that need to be understood in order to communicate effectively in practice. Unfortunately, this basic language of the discipline is sometimes tagged as educational jargon when it is not. Labels and symbols such as *phonological awareness, literal comprehension*, and *scaffolding* are used to refer to precise information specific to literacy learning and instruction that cannot be put in layman's terms and that professionals should use accurately.

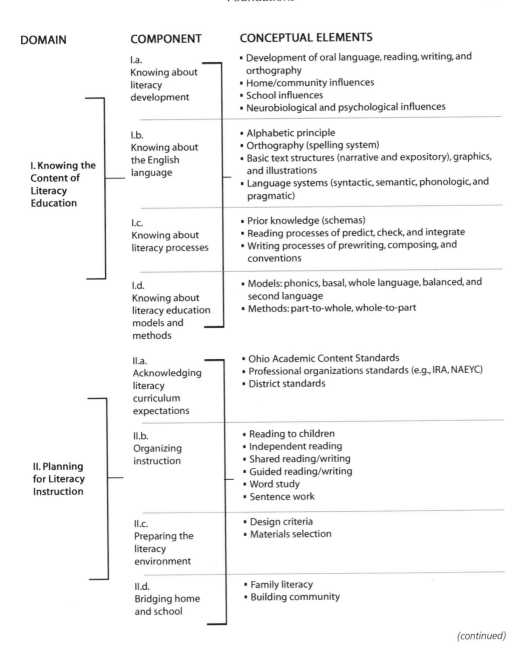

FIGURE 2.2. Core corriculum matrix.

(continued)

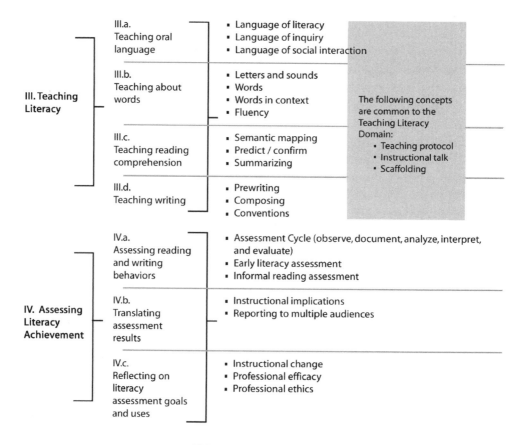

FIGURE 2.2. *(continued)*

Teachers also need to know specific details and facts relevant to the discipline of literacy pedagogy. They should know about events, locations, people, dates, and credible sources of information. Teachers of reading, for example, should know about the National Panel Reading Report (National Reading Panel, 2000) and its significance in the history of reading education. They should be familiar with the work of leading researchers and practitioners in the field, as well as being alert and critical consumers of information about the teaching of reading and writing.

The conceptual knowledge category deals with more complex, organized forms of knowledge that include schemas, mental models, and theories. It involves knowing the classifications and categories of the discipline or how it is structured. Reading, for example, is often organized into three broad categories: word identification, reading comprehension, and strategic knowledge (McKenna & Stahl, 2003). Writing may be organized as process, conventions, and applications.

Conceptual knowledge also deals with the most abstract formulations of the discipline: its theories and models. In literacy pedagogy, this includes knowing about theoretical approaches to understanding the phenomenon (e.g., a Vygotskian view of literacy development or the neurobiology of reading); knowing about instructional approaches (e.g., whole-to-part and part-to-whole approaches) and frameworks (e.g., balanced literacy and guided reading); knowing about research-based instructional sequences (e.g., developing phonological awareness or phonemic manipulation); and other kinds of higher-order, systemic views of the complexities of reading and writing. Teachers need to know these different ways of conceptualizing and organizing literacy pedagogy content and the major areas of inquiry within them (e.g., early literacy, vocabulary processes, sociocultural influences).

The knowing domain interrelates with three other domains: planning, teaching, and assessing. Together they contain conditional knowledge and essential cognitive processes taught in the core curriculum. They address what teachers should know *and* be able to do for effective reading teaching.

The procedural knowledge category has to do with knowing procedures, techniques, and methods that are evidence-based; it involves thinking through steps and sequences for effective application of these methods in instruction. For example, teachers must possess knowledge of the skills needed for decoding so as to provide sequences of instruction that get results. This knowledge type involves knowing when to use specific procedures, techniques, and methods and also involves recognizing the criteria that should be used to make these decisions. In teaching beginning reading, for instance, there are fluency benchmarks that children should meet to develop reading comprehension. Teachers need to know this information and select appropriate interventions when students falter. Teachers need to know enough, in other words, to make good decisions under specific conditions.

Metacognitive knowledge relates to knowing about cognition in general (e.g., learners rely on prior knowledge to gain new knowledge) and knowing about one's own capabilities and teaching strategies. Thinking about thinking (i.e., metacognition), whether in terms of students' learning or one's own learning, is the hallmark of reflective practice wherein teachers are more aware, more strategic, more thoughtful, more deliberate, and therefore more productive in their everyday instruction.

When we use the term *cognitive processes* we are talking about how teachers construct knowledge and transfer what they know to their classroom literacy instruction. Of course, we want teachers to remember and recall what they learn in the core curriculum. But, more so, we want them to understand the content (i.e., the subject matter) well enough to apply it skillfully and to assess its impact on students' literacy development and achievement. This entails a range of higher-order teaching skills that include knowledge construction and generation, analysis, and evaluation based on criteria and standards. As we describe the planning, teaching, and assessing domains more specifically in the following paragraphs, we touch on some of these important processes that drive effective reading and writing instruction.

The planning domain of the core curriculum focuses on the design work of reading and writing instruction. *Design* is an appropriate word to use when talking about instructional planning because it brings out both the artistry and the practicalities of teaching beginning reading. In preparing lessons, teachers must take into account the who, what, how, where, and when of instruction. At the same time, they must keep in mind the desired outcomes of instruction (standards) and the criteria (assessment) they will use to evaluate learner performance. Putting all these elements together into a coherent lesson requires a lot of design skill to create, to organize, to judge, and to construct.

The teaching and assessing domains of the core curriculum address the point at which abstract ideas and plans of instruction are enacted. No professional development curriculum can adequately do justice to the complexities of teaching reading and writing under real conditions. We are teachers and know that, as prepared as we might be, we can never be sure how a lesson will go. We learn to expect the unexpected. Still, there are higher-order teaching skills that lead to more expert teaching, more often under the uncertain conditions of classroom instruction. The core curriculum's teaching and assessing domains target four skill areas that support the development of more powerful higher-order teaching skills. These are (1) using instructional discourse that scaffolds academic learning and promotes positive social interactions in the classroom; (2) carrying out systematic observation and documentation of students' literacy behaviors and achievements; (3) making data-driven instructional decisions; and (4) selecting and implementing theoretically grounded materials that employ research-based approaches and techniques.

Together, the four learning domains of the core curriculum represent a continuous learning model (Figure 2.3) where knowing, planning, teaching, and assessing are interacting elements of an ever-changing and evolving practice (Ulrich, 1997).

Curriculum Components

Looking back at the core curriculum matrix in Figure 2.2, we now focus on the second column, which lists the curricular components of each learning domain. These components of the core curriculum describe the essential ideas of a domain that are fundamental to building an understanding of it. Lacking knowledge about these ideas will make further learning in the domain very difficult. Wiggins and McTighe (1998, p. 10) refer to these basic ideas as "enduring understandings" or what learners must "get inside of" and "carry away with them" so as to learn and continue to learn in the domain.

The core curriculum contains 15 components that represent essential

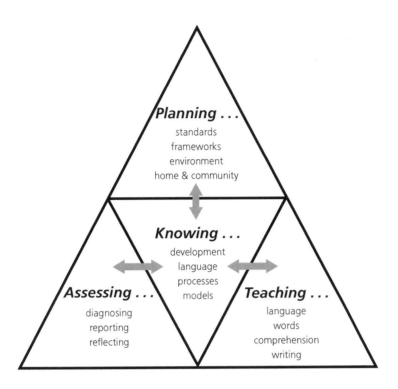

FIGURE 2.3. Model of the core curriculum.

knowledge and skills of primary-grade reading instruction. Certainly there are other important components to be learned. Other professional development curricula might include more of them and also organize them in different ways. Our goal, however, is to offer a "bare-bones" curriculum. It keeps to the basics yet can easily be augmented and deepened to meet the needs of a teacher force diverse in terms of education and experience. Some teachers, for example, hold master's degrees in reading while others have participated in only one reading course as part of their initial preparation. Some are highly experienced primary-grade teachers and some are new beginning teachers. Some have been participating in literacy-related professional development routinely while others have done so only rarely. A leaner curriculum allows more flexibility for adjusting the knowledge base to meet the learning needs of a widely varying teacher audience.

Closer inspection of the components of each domain reveals several strengths of the core curriculum as professional development content. One of these is its multidimensional nature as exemplified in the knowing domain where historical, developmental, sociopsychological, and pedagogic aspects of literacy teaching are discussed. Another strength, reflected in the planning domain, is the curriculum's focus on instructional planning guided by academic content standards, evidence-based approaches, environmental design criteria, and out-of-school factors. An additional major strength is the curriculum's emphasis on systematic, balanced, and data-driven instruction that integrates teacher knowledge and skill toward more expert teaching of reading and writing. The teaching and assessing domains develop the instructional interactions and ongoing assessment skills that create the learning conditions for high student achievement in reading and writing. The components of these domains also stress the importance of professional responsibility and ethics in literacy education as demonstrated in a willingness to reflect on one's teaching, to assume leadership roles, to collaborate, and to strive for personal mastery in one's own practice.

Conceptual Elements

We return once more to the core curriculum matrix in Figure 2.2 and this time look closely at the third column. It lists the major concepts of each curricular component. These concepts are the finer-grained elements within the domain that describe the content to be learned. They are the specifics that bundle together to form the lynchpin ideas of a domain. When unpacked, concepts contain the relevant details, terms, relationships, schemas, and theories that help develop understanding in literacy teaching and learning.

The core curriculum contains 47 conceptual elements that define the 15 curricular components and, in turn, the four learning domains. As with curriculum components, a professional development curriculum may contain many more concepts than these 47, and indeed many professional education curricula do. We selected these 47 because they adequately describe the components of the core curriculum for our stated purpose of a basic curriculum and also offer a manageable number from a practical standpoint given the scope of the LS Project.

Although the conceptual elements specify the components, they still represent rather large chunks of content to be learned. Consider the amount of information, or the "conceptual load," held in ideas, such as the neurobiological and psychological influences on literacy development (knowing domain) or materials selection (planning domain). This, however, is a decided advantage because it allows multiple exposures to the content at different levels of complexity and specificity, which is necessary for reaching a widely diverse teaching force.

In other words, the "grain-size" of the conceptual elements supports differentiated instruction, which may occur within teacher groups or in repeated experiences with the core curriculum at deeper levels of professional development. Teachers, for example, may learn some basic facts of neuroscience that influence general learning in one exposure to the core curriculum, but return later to the same concept, examining more fully what brain-based research means for literacy instruction and the selection of reading interventions. They might learn about research-based reading materials at one time and how to use an evaluation tool to analyze reading materials at another. The conceptual elements, in sum, support ongoing learning in relation to a particular curricular component, and thereby strengthen learning in the entire domain.

Before leaving our discussion of conceptual elements, we draw your attention to three overarching processes of the teaching domain. These are the processes of instructional talk, teaching protocol, and scaffolding. They are interrelated processes because they deal with teacher discourse in the context of instruction—that ability to engage students, convey information, help students think, respond to individual needs, and maintain interest. A teaching protocol is a blueprint for action, such as the steps of a Directed Reading–Thinking Activity (DRTA) (Stauffer, 1975) or Writer's Workshop (Calkins & Harwayne, 1987). Teachers need to learn to execute teaching protocols in reading and writing with accuracy and precision. Teacher and student exchanges bring the protocol to life in the back-and-forth of asking, answering, explaining, clarifying, interpreting, and so forth. To provide expert instruction in key literacy learning areas (oral language, word study, reading comprehension, and writing), teachers must gain mastery of the communication processes that give instruction in any and all literacy areas meaning and value. In so doing, teachers direct students toward more skillful and independent performance. Thus, the core curriculum sets apart these concepts in the teaching domain to ensure that teachers understand and apply these powerful drivers and motivators of learning more deliberately and thoughtfully in practice.

CORE CURRICULUM: WHY IT MATTERS

The core curriculum offers one way to organize the pedagogy of literacy instruction for purposes of sustained professional development in schools. It is evidence-based, orderly, and parsimonious, just as we intended it to be. It makes sense and, as time passes, appears to sustain the LS Project in districts and schools and to support professional learning in other statewide initiatives. But does it really matter?

We think so . . . because a curriculum is more than a framework for organizing professional learning domains, components, and conceptual elements. It is more than a matrix neatly arranged in the columns of a table. It can live as a topic of conversation, an instigator of action, a point of argument, an impetus for change (Applebee, 1996). "Curriculum is not a static entity through which to disseminate knowledge," argues Katie Kinnucan-Welsch, a field faculty member of the LS Project, but rather, "curriculum is an opportunity for discourse and action in which to construct knowledge and understanding" (*The LS Exchange*, Vol. 2, p. 2, 2000).

Beyond its utility as a curriculum scope and sequence, the core curriculum matters because it creates common ground for broad-based discussion among classroom teachers; because it stimulates conversations about professional learning; because it invites teachers to inquire around a set of fundamental ideas; and because it presses them to reason, question, analyze, collaborate, and wonder.

Professional development curricula come and go, and too often leave only traces of change on teachers' everyday practice. We are hopeful that the core curriculum will press more deeply into everyday literacy instruction, and continue to open up thoughtful discourse about literacy teaching and learning among reading educators. We want it to be "a part of practice rather than apart from practice" (*The LS Exchange*, Vol. 2, p. 2, 2000). We want it to be an ongoing conversation about what we know and do in our professional work.

PROFESSIONAL DEVELOPMENT SESSIONS

To widely disseminate a core curriculum for primary-grade educators, we knew it was going to take more than a single document that identifies and explains essential knowledge and processes in literacy pedagogy. Once we reached consensus on the core curriculum among the university reading faculty, we then moved into writing a professional development series that would appeal to higher education faculty, literacy specialists, and teachers. With an eye toward how we could easily translate the series into college coursework for credit, and thereby encourage faculty participation, we developed 15 3-hour learning modules, which we call "professional development sessions." Within each of the four domains of the core curriculum, we brought to life the components and conceptual elements in ways that we hoped would engage teachers in learning more about their craft through their participation in these 15 sessions over a school year. We organized each session into a before–during–after structure to be implemented by a literacy specialist who participates in ongoing training by a field faculty member in the project.

The Professional Developer's Tool

We constructed a tool for the field faculty and literacy specialists to use in presenting the structure, goals, concepts, learning activities, and materials. This tool is a set of 15 trifold session folders. Information that professional developers need to present each session is printed on five panels of the folders. Supplemental readings, transparencies, and activity pages used in each session are inserted in envelopes tucked inside each session folder. Figure 2.4 illustrates the five-panel session folder.

Panel 1
Background Information,
Professional Learning Goals,
Vocabulary

Panel 2
Before: Share, Introduce,
Explain/Show

Panel 3
During: Organize,
Do, Record

Panel 4
After: Present, Discuss,
Summarize, Reflection

Panel 5
Field Work,
Making Connections

FIGURE 2.4. The five-panel core curriculum session folder.

The panel layout for each session folder is similar throughout the sessions and displays session parts that are common to all sessions. Folder panels for Session 1 are shown in Figures 2.5–2.9.

Panel 1: Background Information, Professional Learning Goals, and Vocabulary

Background Information provides an explanation of the key concepts explored in the session. The information is drawn from theory and research and provides the literacy specialist with a knowledge base upon which to launch discussion and exploration of the session topic.

The session part entitled *Professional Learning Goals* identifies what the teachers should know and be able to do through their participation in the sessions. Teachers will *explain*, *interpret*, *apply*, and *reflect* on the session topics as a result of their involvement in session activities. Professional learning goals are stated early in the sessions and used as a tool to determine the effectiveness of the session.

Vocabulary includes the key terms that are defined and used throughout a session to help establish a common language for the discussion and understanding of the topics. The literacy specialists often incorporate effective classroom vocabulary activities, such as word maps or webs, to support teachers' learning and use of the new terms.

Panel 2: Before

Before the presentation of new material, teachers gather in a whole-group setting to share experiences and reflections from the previous session. To introduce the new session, strategies that activate prior knowledge and encourage the teachers to consider their desired learning outcomes are used. The literacy specialist follows with an explain/show segment using transparencies, which are provided in the materials envelope with each session folder.

Panel 3: During

During the session, a problem-solving activity provides the opportunity for teachers to engage in discussion, exploration, interpretation, and application of concepts. The literacy specialist explains the purpose of the activity and directs the teachers to organize into small groups. The small groups then do the activity and record their observations. The activity pages are provided in the materials envelope.

Today a reader, tomorrow a leader. - W. Fusselman

KNOWING ABOUT LITERACY DEVELOPMENT

Background Information

Talking, reading, spelling, and writing are integral processes that begin in the earliest years of life. These are ways children learn to use language to express and receive ideas and to share in the meaning of their worlds. Their use of oral and written language develops as they learn to speak and are involved in the daily routines of family life. Gradually, through the process of talking, children build up practical knowledge of their inherited language systems as they interact with others. Practical knowledge, gained through everyday talk with family members and peers, serves as the foundation of literacy. In turn, the nature of the practical knowledge children acquire is very much influenced by family and peers, along with ethnic, socioeconomic, regional, and cultural differences. The course of children's literacy and biliteracy development is shaped by parental support for talking, reading, spelling, and writing; parents' approaches to literacy and expectations; and the congruence between home and school linguistic environments in the early years of schooling.

Descriptive observations of children's early attempts at talking, writing, spelling, and reading are organized into continuums that reflect the developmental nature of language learning. A continuum makes explicit the phases of written language development and the behaviors that characterize each phase. Teachers can use this information to identify how children are progressing as language users and to inform their planning.

Several different versions of language and literacy development continuums are available. All versions attempt to describe overall developmental patterns that allow for a wide range of individual differences. No two children, it is understood, will follow the same developmental pathways on their way to oral and written language achievement. Some will remain in some phases longer than others, and others may move swiftly through specific phases. The benefit of a continuum is that it provides teachers with a tool to look at what children can do and to plan accordingly for furthering their development. It also alerts educators to the importance of continuity in young children's literacy development and the teacher's role in maintaining that continuity as children move between settings of home, school, and community.

Professional Learning Goals

▲ Explain the continuums of talking, reading, writing, and spelling development.

▲ Interpret individual children's phases of development from observational data.

▲ Apply understanding of development to literacy instruction.

▲ Reflect on application of developmental continuums to planning literacy instruction.

Vocabulary

continuum,
a description of an overall pattern of development.

development,
progressive or regressive changes in shape, size, and function during the lifetime.

language,
the words, sounds, pronunciation, and method of combining words used and understood by people.

literacy,
reading, writing, and the creative and analytical acts involved in producing and comprehending texts.

FIGURE 2.5. Panel 1 of the five-panel core curriculum session folder.

Before

SHARE

Gather the participants together. Discuss the purposes of the professional development series. Review the essential elements of the core (knowledge, skills, and dispositions) and describe how the principles of diagnostic teaching and literacy standards are incorporated into session activities. Review the format of the sessions by explaining the *before-during-after* framework. Discuss the field work assignments and the reflection requirements. Ask the teachers to share their expectations and goals related to the professional development series.

INTRODUCE

Direct the teachers' attention to the topic of the first session – Literacy Development. Review the Diagnostic Process (T1.1) and highlight how careful observation of students and assessment of literacy concepts and skills guides planning and instruction. Ask them to tell what they know about young children's developing literacy concepts and skills. Record their ideas and observations on a transparency or piece of chart paper. Next, have the teachers tell what they would like to know about the literacy development of young children. Record their questions as before. Overview the session activities which focus on key features of literacy development.

Note: This is a K-W-L activity that records what teachers already know about the topic and what they want to know. They will explore what they learned about the topic following the activity and again when they reflect in a personal log or journal.

EXPLAIN/SHOW

Explain that as students mature as readers and writers, they exhibit overall patterns of development in oral language, reading, writing, and spelling. Present the developmental continuums (T1.2-1.4). Discuss them in relation to teachers' comments previously recorded in the KWL activity. Examine the behavioral characteristics in relation to the concepts and skills that are developing. Tell the teachers that they will examine literacy development by looking carefully at samples of talking, reading, writing, and spelling of emergent readers to become familiar with the continuums. Show the transparency series (T1.5-1.7). Prompt teachers to make observations about the samples. Use the guiding questions to focus teachers' observations. Next, show the connection between what the student knows and needs to learn. The learning expectations are the ELA Standards, Benchmarks, and Grade-level Indicators. Return to the emergent writing sample (T1.8) and guide the teachers' comparison of the student's writing development with the Kindergarten Indicators for the Writing Applications and Writing Conventions Standards.

EMERGENT
(approximately ages 3-5)

EARLY/BEGINNING
(ages 5-7)

TRANSITIONAL
(ages 7-8)

INTERMEDIATE/ADVANCED
(ages 8+)

KIT MATERIALS:

Transparencies: T1.1 – T1.8
Activity Packet: A1.1 – A1.10
Field Work: FW1.1
Learning Modules CD 1,
   Domain I: Knowing

LOCAL MATERIALS:

Ohio K-12 English Language Arts Standards

Samples of students' reading and writing

Know	Want to Know	Learned

BRIGHT STARTERS

To spark interest in the session, read a picture book about growing-up, such as *Growing Pains* by Jenny Stow or *Leo the Late Bloomer* by Robert Kraus.

FIGURE 2.6. Panel 2 of the five-panel core curriculum session folder.

During

PROBLEM-SOLVING ACTIVITY: Watching Readers and Writers Grow

ORGANIZE

Have the teachers form small groups of 3-4 per group. Tell them that they will examine oral language, reading, writing, and spelling samples, then identify Standards and Grade-level Indicators that align with what the student knows and needs to learn. The purpose of this activity is to extend and consolidate what they know about the developmental phases of literacy. Emphasize that knowledge of literacy development is critical for diagnostic teaching of reading and writing.

DO

Give a packet of literacy samples to each group (A1.1, A1.2 – 1.10). Ask the teachers to choose one set of samples to examine (early/beginning, transitional, or intermediate/advanced). Next, tell them to choose a sample from the set to compare to the Reading and Writing Standards. Ask them to identify Indicators at a particular grade level most closely aligned with what the student knows and needs to learn.

RECORD

Tell the teachers to record their observations of literacy behaviors and explain how they relate to the Standards and Indicators.

	TALKING	READING	WRITING	SPELLING
EMERGENT (AGES 3-5)				
EARLY/BEGINNING (AGES 5-7)				
TRANSITIONAL (AGES 7-8)				
INTERMEDIATE/ADVANCED (AGES 8+)				

"Although human beings have been living and dying for millions of years, they have been writing for only six thousand years."

Rene Etiemble

BOOKSHELF

Bransford, J., Brown, A., & Cocking, R. (Eds.). (2000). *How people learn: Brain, mind, experience, and school.* Washington, DC: National Academy Press.

Burns, M. S., Griffin, P., & Snow, C. E. (Eds.). (1999). *Starting out right: A guide to promoting children's reading success.* Washington, DC: National Academy Press.

Meek, M. (1984). *Learning to read.* Portsmouth, NH: Heinemann Educational Books.

Schickendanz, J. (1999). *Much more than the ABCs.* Washington, DC: National Association for the Education of Young Children.

Temple, C., Nathan, R., Temple, F., & Burris, N. (1993). *The beginnings of writing* (3rd ed.). Boston, MA: Allyn & Bacon.

FIGURE 2.7. Panel 3 of the five-panel core curriculum session folder.

Panel 4: After

To complete the before–during–after session framework, the teachers reconvene as a whole group to present and discuss their small-group work, building on the previous group's presentation. The literacy specialist summarizes the information by reviewing the session content and recalling the teachers' experiences and small-group activities. Together they resolve any unanswered questions. Teachers then reflect on new learning as stated in the professional learning goals of the session. They are asked to think back on the session and respond to various prompts in a personal log or journal.

Panel 5: Field Work and Making Connections

Field Work is an activity that requires the teachers to apply new concepts and skills to local contexts of district, school, and classroom. The opportunity to extend learning through activities that take place in an authentic setting using materials of practice is embedded in the professional learning goals of each session. *Field Work* activity pages state the purpose and provide directions. At the next session, teachers are expected to share and discuss their *Field Work* experiences.

Making Connections, like *Field Work*, describes activities that extend beyond the session and provide relevant and meaningful learning experiences linked to practice. Teachers work alone, with partners, in small groups, or with a literacy specialist to carry out these activities. Less structured than *Field Work* in design, *Making Connections* presents scenarios or problems of practice that aim to stretch teachers to think more about and act upon what they have learned in the professional development session.

Given that the session folder is the primary tool for disseminating the core curriculum, we interspersed other design features across the five panels to enhance learning opportunities in the sessions:

- *Graphics*: charts, diagrams, or pictures to highlight or illustrate session content.
- *Quotations*: words to stimulate thinking about teaching and learning.
- *Kit Materials*: a list of materials to use in the session.
- *Local Materials*: a list of teaching or learning artifacts, such as student work, report cards, and teacher guides, to make session activities more authentic for participants.
- *Bright Starters*: children's book titles to spark interest in the sessions and introduce children's literature. (A complete list of *Bright Starters* for each session is included in Figure 2.10.)

After

PRESENT

Draw the groups together for a discussion of activity results. Ask each group to present its findings. Tell each group to build on the previous group's presentation.

> "Language is for using, and the uses of language are so varied, so rich, and each use so preemptive a way of life, that to study it is to study the world and indeed, all possible worlds."
>
> Jerome Bruner

DISCUSS

Emphasize the key features observed in each phase of development. Relate these back to the teachers' earlier ideas about literacy development. Note any new information and insights. Discuss the questions that teachers asked early on in the session and, to the extent possible, answer them. Emphasize how diagnostic teaching takes into account student's development, systematic observation of reading and writing behaviors, and learning expectations (standards). Choose one or more observations from the activity to use for a discussion about how the observational data guide planning and instruction for teaching comprehension, fluency, vocabulary, phonemic awareness, writing, phonics, and oral language.

SUMMARIZE

Draw the session to a close by re-examining the continuums of oral language (T1.2), reading (T1.3), writing, and orthographic word knowledge (T1.4). Review the features of development in each phase. Recall observations from experience and from the small group activity. Highlight key features and themes. Resolve any remaining questions that the teachers have.

REFLECTION

Take a moment to reflect about this session.
Respond to the following prompts in your personal log or journal.

SUMMARY: a brief description of the key points

NEW LEARNING: major new insights that come out of the session for you

QUESTIONS: questions that emerge from the topics, issues, or strategies

PERSONAL: a personal reaction to the context, content, or strategies used

▸ SUMMARY ▸ NEW LEARNING ▸ QUESTIONS ▸ PERSONAL REACTION

WORTH A LOOK

View two videos about child development and brain research:

"The Secret Life of the Brain". PBS Series.
Available from www.pbs.org

"Ready to Learn" hosted by Jamie Lee Curtis and LeVar Burton
Available from I Am Your Child Organization:
www.iamyourchild.org/order

FIGURE 2.8. Panel 4 of the five-panel core curriculum session folder.

Field Work

PURPOSE: To examine literacy samples from a developmental perspective to determine what students know and need to learn (FW1.1).

DIRECTIONS

Collect oral language, reading, and writing samples from one student.

Study the samples from a developmental perspective and record observations.

Identify the appropriate Standard and Grade-level Indicators that most closely align with what the student knows and needs to learn.

Choose one area of need and design an instructional strategy to enhance the student's literacy development.

Record your analysis on the chart and outline an instructional strategy on the reverse side.

Observations of literacy characteristics:	Use the samples to identify appropriate Standard and Grade-level Indicators that most closely align with what the student knows and needs to learn. Grade Level_____
Oral Language	Standard:
	Indicator(s):
Reading	Standard:
	Indicator(s):
Writing	Standard:
	Indicator(s):
Spelling	Standard:
	Indicator(s):

MAKING CONNECTIONS

You have been invited to make a presentation on literacy development at a district-wide parent meeting. Provide an outline of the main points of your talk.

COMING UP

Next session:
KNOWING ABOUT THE ENGLISH LANGUAGE

• Explore three basic elements of the English language as a writing system.

• Interpret how these basic elements characterize written English.

• Reflect on the importance of knowing the English language on early literacy instruction.

FIGURE 2.9. Panel 5 of the five-panel core curriculum session folder.

Introduction
Mrs. Spitzer's Garden by Edith Pattou

Session 1
Leo the Late Bloomer by Robert Kraus
Growing Pains by Jenny Stow

Session 2
The Journey of English by Donna Brook

Session 3
Drawing Lessons from a Bear by David
McPhail

Session 4
McGuffey's Eclectic Readers by William Holmes
McGuffey

Session 5
Testing Miss Malarkey by Judy Finchler

Session 6
The Awful Aardvarks Shop for School
by Reeve Lindbergh

Session 7
There's a Zoo in Room 22 by Judy Sierra

Session 8
Arthur's Teacher Moves In by Marc Brown

Session 9
Elbert's Bad Word by Audrey Wood

Session 10
Miss Alaineus: A Vocabulary Disaster by Debra
Frasier

Session 11
Thank You, Mr. Falkner by Patricia Polacco

Session 12
What Do Authors Do? by Eileen Christelow

Session 13
Arthur's Teacher Trouble by Marc Brown

Session 14
Teach Us, Amelia Bedelia by Peggy Parish

Session 15
Horray for Diffendoofer Day! by Dr. Seuss

FIGURE 2.10. *Bright Starters* for each session.

- *Bookshelf*: a list of professional books to provide additional information on session topics.
- *Worth a Look*: a list of video and Internet resources to provide additional information on session topics.
- *Coming Up*: a preview of the professional learning goals for the next session to pique interest and allow participants to plan ahead.

CLOSING

Together the state's conceptual framework and the core curriculum give legitimacy to the LS Project. Because the project is situated in a broad-based conceptual framework (i.e., the Ohio Literacy Initiative), it is included in the larger agenda of educational reform, which has implications for ongoing funding and integration into related projects. This helps to stabilize the project when faced with the challenges of larger-scale implementation. That it has a core curriculum identifies the project's position, where it stands as a professional development model. And its position helps to establish its credibility and brings coherence to the many-layered activities from conceptual to practical levels that support effective professional development for teachers.

We point out here, as we did in the Introduction, that the professional development session is an activity setting, wherein professionals come together around a shared goal of learning more and developing more skill as literacy educators. Each session, which examines a key topic and conceptual elements of the core curriculum, is designed to create an integrated professional learning experience that is both goal- and participant-driven, and creates much-needed opportunities for coming to mutual understanding through collaboration.

In the next chapter, we introduce the network system that is used to disseminate the core curriculum to multiple sites throughout the state. We define the triadic structure of the learning network and describe the roles and responsibilities of the key players as they go about their work of providing professional development in the LS Project.

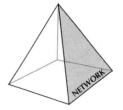

CHAPTER 3

Organization

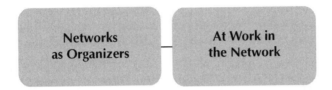

We are charting new ground and discovering new ways to make [statewide] professional development a teacher-centered learning opportunity. Your participation in this work is important, as well as your input.

—*The LS Exchange* (Vol. 2, p. 1, 2000)

All large-scale endeavors, whether distributing food, vaccine, or new knowledge, are faced with the problem of garnering and deploying sufficient resources to get the job done efficiently and well. Putting a statewide professional development program in reading into place is no exception in this regard. One of the most challenging problems we faced in the LS Project was how to deliver the professional development model to thousands of teachers across the state in a way that was consistent with the core curriculum yet responsive to local needs. Our solution to this problem, the topic of this chapter, is revealed through a description of the committed professional developers and providers who bring the LS Project to life.

We begin by introducing you to the concept of a network system, which we used to organize and disseminate the professional development model. A network system offers an organizational structure that links together state agencies, universities, and schools. We then describe key roles and responsibilities in the delivery of the professional development model from the state education agency to the schools. We show how these roles and responsibilities interrelate to form small learning networks within the system and how these networks, in turn, help to build institutional capacity for improving reading instruction. We know that, as readers, you bring diverse experiences to this information, so we invite you to examine the composition and functions of our network system through your particular lenses as professional development planner, designer, provider, participant, or policymaker. We hope in doing so you will gain insights not only about your own current role, but also new perspectives about the human resources needed to widely disseminate quality professional development.

NETWORKS AS ORGANIZERS

A *network* is a pattern of organization that supports relationships among its members so as to realize a purpose or goal. In this sense, a network is similar to a book club or a study group. But it is also different in that a network system is held accountable for getting results. A network system, in short, coordinates relationships (the means) to realize a larger purpose, function, or goal (the results) and holds relationships to this purpose (Capra, 1996). In this respect, it relies on both process and accountability elements.

Given the state's goal for the LS Project—to disseminate professional development based on a core curriculum to many teachers in many schools—a network system offered a promising way to organize for two reasons. One, networks could tap the human resources in universities, colleges, and schools across the state that might contribute to the effort. Two, networks could channel this collective expertise to the implementation of the core curriculum as the basis of professional development in literacy instruction.

Using this approach in the LS Project, we developed a network system that includes university and college reading faculty (referred to as "field faculty members"), district- or school-based reading specialists (referred to as "literacy specialists"), and classroom teachers. Each year, through state-funded grants to universities and colleges, field faculty members are recruited to work with 15–20 literacy specialists, who are supported in this role by their local school districts. Literacy specialists, in turn, deliver professional development sessions based on the core curriculum to small groups of 15–20 classroom teachers. Once operational, the network system disseminates professional development on a large scale. Figure 3.1 depicts this triadic structure of the learning networks. Such a network system can work not only for sustained professional development in primary-grade reading instruction, but also for professional development in

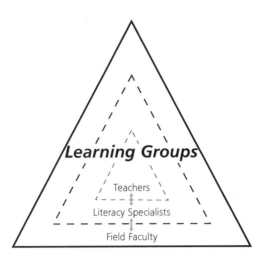

FIGURE 3.1. Triadic structure of learning networks.

other disciplines (e.g., math), as well as for other levels of professional literacy education (e.g., adolescent literacy).

While this network structure resembles the familiar "trainer of trainers" model (Loucks-Horsley, Hewson, Love, & Stiles, 1998) so often used in large-scale professional development, it has several unique features. Each professional learning context (field faculty members with each other, field faculty members with their respective literacy specialist groups, and literacy specialists with their respective teacher groups) functions as an activity setting wherein people in their particular roles (field faculty, literacy specialist, or classroom teacher) come together regularly around a shared goal and assist the performance of each other in achieving the goal (Tharp & Gallimore, 1988). A network in this sense (and what makes it unique) includes cognitive components, such as planning and problem solving, as well as external, social components, such as times and places for professional development activity. What happens in these activity settings is goal-driven. For example, what people do and why they do it is shaped by the goals of activity (e.g., learning research-based reading instruction methods). But at the same time, as people work together, the meaning of the activity continues "to develop, to emerge, to explain, and to perpetuate" (Tharp & Gallimore, 1988, p. 73). Therefore, what happens is dynamic, not static, influenced by an invisible spectrum of ecocultural factors and also shaped by the intersubjectivity of the participants at hand. Stated more simply, networks support the formation of professional learning groups that are in ongoing communication with one another. The dialogue and problem solving that occur within and between them create opportunities for professional learning that is both individual and shared with colleagues. Their interactions also provide feedback on how well the LS Project is working, thus holding it and its participants accountable for achieving its stated goals. (In Chapter 7, we explain accountability in the LS Project.)

In the LS Project, the entire field faculty meets monthly with the project director. At these full-day meetings, a variety of activities take place around agenda items that focus each meeting. The meetings often begin with the field faculty discussing a common set of readings they selected to advance their own knowledge of core curriculum-related topics (e.g., neurological research on reading, English language learning and development, assessment). Field faculty members also preview and discuss videos that they will present in their meetings with literacy specialists, who, in turn, present in their professional development sessions with teachers. These discussions typically heat up to strong intellectual discussion or debate and then boil down to everyone gaining new insights about teaching and learning. For example, in their discussion of the video *Reciprocal Teaching Strategies at Work: Improving Reading Comprehension, Grades 2–6* (International Reading Association and Lamplight Media, 2003), field faculty members commented both on the video content and pedagogical issues related to what literacy specialists and teachers need to know to implement the strategy. Some critical points recorded in the March 2006 field faculty meeting notes included:

> The "reciprocal" wasn't evident very much in the video, but it does remind the viewer that it is the teacher and the students implementing the strategy—not just the students.

> The teachers did a good job of teaching teachers how to implement reciprocal teaching and modeling the strategy, but they could have let the students talk more.

> There seemed to be a lack of information in the video as to who needs reciprocal teaching. It is most likely the case that all students can benefit from the strategy at their level—for example, proficient readers would need to use challenging texts.

Other comments related to their need to critique the video with their literacy specialists and raise questions to deepen their understanding of the strategy.

> We need to get the literacy specialists and teachers to take what they see in the video to a deeper level. The goal is that students need to demonstrate the use of these metacognitive processes on their own. We need to discuss questions such as, "Do you assess students as to whether they need reciprocal teaching?" "Would this strategy help a proficient reader?" and "How do you know where students are?"

> Teachers need to understand reciprocal teaching and teach all of the individual strategies separately, and they need to provide enough modeling and practice until they know that their students can use the strategies independently.

At these monthly meetings, field faculty members also share ideas and brainstorm a great deal about how to more efficiently organize their meetings with literacy specialists, how to help the literacy specialists present the core curriculum sessions to engage teachers and keep them engaged in learning new content, and how to solve problems the literacy specialists face at the schools (e.g., resolving scheduling conflicts). These once-a-month meeting activities create and sustain a professional learning context for this reading faculty, who, in turn, carry the professional development forward to their respective groups of literacy specialists.

Following the field faculty–director meetings during the school year, each field faculty member meets monthly with their literacy specialists for a full day of professional development, usually held in a university or conference center. Field faculty members, as professional developers, guide in-depth study of the core curriculum content. They model and discuss ways that literacy specialists can engage classroom teachers in learning and applying core curriculum concepts and skills to their own practice. Teachers want to be actively involved and to have their ideas recognized and validated. Field faculty members model the use of K–W–L, Think–Pair–Share, Grand Conversation, and other strategies that are applicable to classroom instruction. Together with the literacy specialists, they reflect on their own engagement and motivation and discuss how these strategies are likely to work in their teacher sessions. On the heels of these monthly meetings, the literacy specialists follow through by providing approximately 3 hours of school-based professional development every other week to their classroom teacher groups in school settings.

Roles and Responsibilities

Efficient and effective implementation of the statewide professional development model of the LS Project depends on people who are informed and committed to the work. This requires a clear sense of the differentiated roles and responsibilities that contribute to a successful model of professional development. In the following sections, we sketch the roles and responsibilities of the key players in the LS Project. Readers may find these sketches helpful in defining their roles in professional development and considering others that may be needed in planning future professional development endeavors.

Field Faculty

Affiliated with universities and colleges, field faculty members prepare literacy specialists for teaching the core curriculum content (the basis of professional development) and for coaching classroom teachers toward more skillful practice. A typical monthly meeting of a field faculty member and literacy specialists includes a walk-through of one or more upcoming professional development

sessions that the literacy specialists will teach. Each field faculty member orga-
nizes his or her literacy specialists into small groups to plan and practice teaching parts of the sessions. Through these rehearsals, the literacy specialists collaboratively plan ways to organize the teachers, use the materials, and sequence
the learning activities. They have numerous opportunities to articulate and clar-
ify key concepts, experience the activities themselves, anticipate teachers' questions, trouble-shoot potential difficulties, raise issues, and problem solve. After
these small-group presentations, the literacy specialists self- and peer assess
their presentations. They reflect on what worked and what did not work, and
they think ahead to what will work best with their own teacher groups. In their
ongoing collaboration with their field faculty member, the literacy specialists
deepen their content knowledge, develop skills in teaching adults, and cultivate
the dispositions expected of professional teacher educators. In general, the
professional development provided by the field faculty to literacy specialists
attempts to model the kind of quality professional development that literacy specialists should offer teachers. The primary responsibilities associated with the
field faculty role include:

- Participate in monthly professional development meetings with the direc-
  tor.
- Provide input on the core curriculum sessions.
- Provide monthly training sessions on the core curriculum to literacy spe-
  cialists.
- Assist and advise the literacy specialists in the organization of the profes-
  sional development sessions at the school level.
- Conduct observations of the literacy specialists' professional development
  sessions with teachers.
- Use observational data to guide the ongoing professional development of
  literacy specialists.
- Establish and maintain a communication network within and between the
  literacy specialist–teacher groups.
- Arrange for graduate credit course offerings for literacy specialists and
  teachers.
- Participate in research and evaluation activities.
- Provide monthly reports on implementation to the project director.

Meeting these responsibilities takes considerable time and effort on the part
of each field faculty member. Although they have a 6-hour day each month to
spend with the literacy specialists, they need to be well planned so they do not
get sidetracked for too long on local issues, such as difficulties with scheduling
professional development sessions, or finding time and ways to communicate
progress of the professional development to administrators and others. In the
ebb and flow of school life, professional development sessions may need to be

postponed, and finding another meeting time requires coordination and cooperation among the teachers and the administrators. These and other problems of
implementation are shared. Still, this problem-solving time is only part of the
meeting. The field faculty must spend considerable time and effort in planning
to assure that the monthly meetings also afford ample time to develop the literacy specialists' knowledge and skills so they can successfully implement their
professional development sessions with teachers.

Literacy Specialists

Literacy specialists are employees of the school districts (e.g., Title I teachers,
classroom teachers, language arts coordinators) who participate in the project.
Some literacy specialists teach children all day; some teach children part of the
day; and others do not have any teaching responsibilities. Literacy specialists typically conduct their professional development sessions after school hours.

The literacy specialists' positions within the district largely determine the
type and frequency of professional development activities they may provide to
teachers. The roles and responsibilities of the literacy specialists in the LS Project
align with those outlined in the International Reading Association's (2004b)
position statement on coaching (see Figure 3.2).

Literacy specialists who are full-time teachers with no time during their regular schedule to observe in classrooms or coach teachers typically engage in
informal Level 1 coaching activities defined in the position statement. For example, they have conversations about practice with colleagues, help develop or
provide instructional materials, participate in conferences or workshops with
other colleagues, assist with assessments, and lead study groups, such as the
professional development sessions in the LS Project.

Literacy specialists with part-time teaching responsibilities engage in more
formal and somewhat more intense Level 2 coaching activities. In addition to
teaching the core curriculum to colleagues, they may lead grade-level meetings,
assist teachers by coplanning lessons, and have individual conferences with
teachers about assessment and instruction.

Literacy specialists who serve full time in the capacity of professional developer engage in the formal and more intense Level 3 coaching activities. In addition to teaching the core curriculum to colleagues, they model and discuss lessons, observe instruction and provide feedback to teachers, and analyze with
teachers audio- or videotaped lessons of classroom instruction.

In all cases, the literacy specialists, when fully or partially serving in the role
of literacy specialist, provide professional development sessions focused on the
core curriculum to a group of teachers in their school or district throughout the
year. One of the challenges for those not teaching children all or part of the day
is that their administrators may assign them to other time-consuming duties
(e.g., coordinating schoolwide literacy events), which take them away from pro-

Level 1 Coaching Activities (informal; helps to develop relationships)	Level of Literacy Specialist Participation
• Conversations with colleagues (identifying issues or needs, setting goals, problem solving) • Developing and providing materials for/with colleagues • Participating in professional development activities with colleagues (conferences, workshops) • Leading or participating in study groups • Assisting with assessing students • Instructing students to learn about their strengths and needs	• Full-time teaching • Facilitates core curriculum sessions • No release time to provide individualized assistance to teachers
Level 2 Coaching Activities (more formal; begins to look at areas of need and focus)	Level of Literacy Specialist Participation
• Coplanning lessons • Holding team meetings (grade level, reading teachers) • Analyzing student work • Interpreting assessment data (helping teachers use results for instructional decision making) • Individual discussions with colleagues about teaching and learning • Making professional development presentations to teachers	• Some teaching • Facilitates core curriculum sessions throughout the school year • Some release time to provide individualized assistance to teachers
Level 3 Coaching Activities (formal, more intense; may create some anxiety on the part of teacher or coach)	Level of Literacy Specialist Participation
• Modeling and discussing lessons • Coteaching lessons • Visiting classrooms and providing feedback to teachers • Analyzing videotaped lessons of teachers • Doing lesson study with teachers	• No teaching • Facilitates core curriculum sessions throughout the school year • Full release time to provide individualized assistance to teachers

FIGURE 3.2. Coaching activities at different levels of literacy specialist participation. Data from International Reading Association (2004b).

viding individualized support to classroom teachers. In some cases, the field faculty member provides one-on-one assistance to the literacy specialist in how to better manage time and tasks, and how to communicate the role and responsibilities to the administration. The field faculty member may also join the literacy specialist in this kind of communication with administrators. The literacy specialists also assist one another during their monthly meetings by sharing what has worked for them in similar situations.

An excerpt from the LS Project's newsletter, *The LS Exchange*, illustrates a "day in the life" of Terry, a literacy specialist who spends some of her day teaching students and other parts of the day engaged in professional development work (see Figure 3.3). As you follow Terry's account, you will notice how her activities dovetail with those listed for Levels 1, 2, and 3 of the International Reading Association's (2004b) position statement.

Teachers

Unlike traditional venues of professional development, the professional development model offered through the LS Project requires sustained engagement with the content and the application of research-based practices in reading and writing instruction. For the teachers, this entails making a commitment to themselves, their colleagues, and their school community to join a professional learning community.

At the outset of a new year in the LS Project, we share the expectation that participation means not only attending all 15 core curriculum sessions but also following through with *Field Work* and *Making Connections* extensions to spark interest in leading literacy efforts at schoolwide meetings and other functions. At the introductory session, the literacy specialist overviews the core curriculum and gives teachers a taste of the content and learning activities that they will participate in throughout the upcoming year. The literary specialist also presents and discusses the Memorandum of Understanding (Figure 3.4) which sets forth the expectations for participation in the LS Project. Nearly all who attend that opening session will indicate their commitment by signing the memorandum. Others will decide that it is not an opportune time for the required long-term involvement. We recognize that even when teachers do sign the memorandum, not all of them will participate fully, with 100% attendance and implementation of the extension activities that follow each session. Some will have unforeseen circumstances arise to prevent them from attending a session; others will have the best intentions but other priorities will take precedence. Still, we do expect that a commitment needs to be articulated and recognized at the outset (and, once in a while, as a reminder) if a learning community is going to be established and sustained. (We will say more about accountability with respect to roles of individuals in Chapter 7.)

A Day in the Life...

A typical day in my professional life as a literacy specialist begins between 8-8:30 a.m. First I check my schedule in the office to see what I have on my plate for the day. The schedule is a sign-up sheet where teachers write the time and jot down notes to guide my work with them. They will typically sign-up for one-on-one meetings with me, class lessons, and/or individual assessments of children referred for IAT (Intervention Assistant Team) meetings. I then begin the appointments on my schedule. If I don't have anyone signed up for one-on-one at 8:30 (school starts at 9:10), I use the time to check e-mail and voice mail and reply to the many messages I receive. I usually schedule my lunch at a time when I can talk with teachers. Most days, this is the only chance we have to talk. I try to allow myself one planning period each day. The rest of the afternoon, I conduct assessments or teach lessons. If I ever have a slow day (which isn't often), I use the time to catch up on locating and distributing resource materials. Not unlike my literacy specialist colleagues, I often stay well after school to attend meetings or just to catch up on the myriad of things I have promised to do.

> Level 3:
> modeling and discussing lessons

> Level 1:
> providing materials for colleagues

One of my primary responsibilities as a literacy specialist has been to provide support and professional development to staff and administrators. To this end, I offer the core curriculum sessions and other workshops district-wide. Most of the sessions focus on best literacy practices. I provide training to high school students and community volunteers (including parents) who tutor in OhioReads (community volunteer program). When I'm not providing training, I collaborate with consultants on staff development to support our new literacy program. I help classroom, special education, and Title I teachers make the best use of our new reading series and other resources, and to learn about new teaching techniques.

> Level 2:
> making professional development presentations to teachers

While training and professional development are my primary job functions, the service that I provide daily to students and teachers is also of great importance. Two primary services that I provide are: (1) assessment and diagnosis of students' reading performance and (2) work with children individually, in small groups and within the whole class environment. I often participate in IAT meetings to present assessment findings and to make recommendations for accommodations, further instruction, and/or educational program placement. I also conduct screenings on children that are new to our district so that the teacher can obtain valuable information, which can help guide instruction for that child.

> Level 1:
> · assisting with assessing students
> · instructing students to learn about their strengths and needs

FIGURE 3.3. A day in the life of a literacy specialist. From *The LS Exchange* (Vol. 11, p. 6, 2002).

Further, the commitment to participate fully in the professional development underscores the disposition goals in the core curriculum. Professional educators are expected to:

- Make a commitment to reflect on one's teaching performance.
- Contribute to a learning community of classroom, school, family, and profession.
- Collaborate with others.
- Strive for personal mastery.
- Take responsibility for understanding and adapting to change in literacy education.

LITERACY SPECIALIST PROJECT

Memorandum of Understanding: Teacher

Faculty from 13 Ohio universities, over 200 literacy specialists, and roughly 1,600 teachers are expected to participate in the statewide professional development initiative centered on a core curriculum for educators in 2004-2005. As literacy educators, we face both exciting opportunities and serious challenges in our daily professional work. For all who participate, we have a unique opportunity to develop our profession and to meet the challenge of bringing all children to literacy.

The success of this large-scale effort can only be realized through each person's commitment to it. Your participation will afford opportunities to learn more about your literacy teaching, receive professional reading materials and resources, and experience the satisfaction of professional learning.

The **Teacher** agrees to
- collaborate with the literacy specialist in coaching activities to improve teaching.
- engage in collaborative inquiry with colleagues.
- complete all readings and field work for each session.
- participate in research and evaluation activities.
- take responsibility for improving teaching to enhance children's literacy achievement.

Please sign below to indicate your intention to participate fully in this initiative.

Teacher (please print)	Teacher's Signature	Date
Principal (please print)	Principal's Signature	Date
School District	School	

FIGURE 3.4. Memorandum of Understanding for teacher.

For many teachers, this commitment to continuous professional learning is natural. When they transport new ideas from professional development to their practice, they get enthused about their craft and motivated to talk about their discoveries, insights, and reflections about what works and what does not work so well in teaching, and what they can do to improve student achievement. This is the nature of discussion that builds and sustains a professional learning community committed to growth in all of its members.

Administrators

Just as the field faculty, literacy specialists, and teachers make a commitment when they form a professional learning community in the LS Project, it is equally important that school administrators recognize their role in supporting the literacy specialists and teachers who devote a lot of time and effort to year-long professional development. Several ways that principals support the project include:

- Assist with recruiting teachers to participate in the professional development.
- Facilitate the literacy specialist's teaching of the core curriculum and other coaching activities by arranging for space, scheduling, supplies, and the like.
- Communicate support of the literacy specialist and teachers participating in the project to others in the school community.
- Provide release time for the literacy specialist to attend monthly professional development meetings with the field faculty member.
- Facilitate the literacy specialist's involvement in other various professional development opportunities—for example, national, state, and regional conferences.

AT WORK IN THE NETWORK

Each group within the network system (project director with the field faculty, field faculty members with literacy specialists, literacy specialists with teachers) bears a responsibility for the successful implementation of each and every professional development session at the local school level. It is this collective sense of responsibility that fosters conditions for professional learning and also establishes accountability for getting the desired results. It is first cultivated *within* the groups and then *between* groups as members share their learning experiences.

A brief look inside the different groups shows how individuals in their respective roles prepare and motivate themselves and others for the professional development sessions. In the process, they assume responsibility for professional learning at all levels of program implementation.

In their monthly meetings, field faculty members prepare to assist literacy specialists through collaborative inquiry with other field faculty members and through their own independent study. They jointly plan how to assist literacy specialists in acquiring new literacy content knowledge and pedagogical knowledge about how to teach reading effectively. Field faculty member Kay Milkie remarks:

The [project director–field faculty] meetings allow many opportunities for sharing ideas, concerns, materials, and stories with colleagues. As we work together through each professional development session, we are able to take a close look at the content and the accompanying materials. We continually push each other out of our comfort zones as we grapple with ways to organize meaningful and worthwhile learning activities for each session. (*The LS Exchange*, Vol. 6, p. 4, 2001)

Her comments indicate the field faculty's deliberate attention to the integrity of the professional development content and its effort in ensuring that it is current, relevant, and delivered in a way that enhances teacher thinking. The meeting agenda shown in Figure 3.5 is an illustration of the content and goals of the field faculty's work.

When literacy specialists meet with their field faculty member, their overarching goal is to design ways to create and sustain a strong learning community with their respective teacher groups. All teacher groups share common concerns and needs (e.g., how to organize instruction based on assessment data), but each also has its unique concerns, needs, learning preferences, and proclivities. Through the network system, literacy specialists learn ways to create shared understandings across teacher groups and at the same time learn how to meet the specific needs and address the specific issues of individual teacher groups. They read to learn more; they study the professional development session content under the guidance of their field faculty member and on their own; they spend time thinking through and organizing authentic learning activities; they remain open to others' ideas and accept critiques from others. Amy, a literacy specialist, relates:

The experience of being a literacy specialist is an invaluable one. I've been able to build professional relationships and learn from others' personal and professional experience. Teaching the core curriculum has given me practice in front of my peers and has given me confidence in my own growth as an educator. The knowledge I've gained from the regional meetings and from the teachers in my group has lifted my teaching to a higher level. (*The LS Exchange*, Vol. 6, p. 4, 2001)

Like the director's meetings with field faculty, the field faculty meetings with literacy specialists are well planned and focused on learning and working out ways to best implement the core curriculum. The meeting agenda shown in Figure 3.6 further illustrates the content and goals of the literacy specialists' work.

Guided and encouraged (and even inspired) by their literacy specialists, classroom teachers are prepared to learn in their small groups, motivated by the powerful goal of helping their own students read well. Hopes for our students can be powerful motivators to change our own practices, even though it may be

FIELD FACULTY MEETING
MARCH 10, 2006
9:00 AM TO 3:00 PM

Recorder: Judy Patburg

Location: Holiday Inn, Worthington

Agenda

9:00 – 9:15   Continental breakfast and announcements

9:15 – 10:45   Resource Preview: Reciprocal Teaching

10:45 – 12:00   Discussion of Reading
                      Chapters 1 and 6 in *Knowledge to Support the Teaching of Reading*
                      (Snow, Griffin, & Burns, 2005)

12:00 – 12:45   LUNCH

12:45 – 2:45   LS Conference Planning
                      Meeting Structure
                      Field Work Analysis

2:45 - 3:00   Wrap-Up

Bring:
Laptop   (optional, not used for internet)
Field Work samples

Materials to be Distributed to Field Faculty:
Article from "The Columbus Dispatch"

Future Meetings
 • *Next Field Faculty meeting – April 14, Holiday Inn, Worthington*

FIGURE 3.5. Field faculty meeting agenda.

at times difficult and painful to give up familiar ways. Second-grade teacher Keli, for example, takes steps to prepare for each upcoming session. She explains, "I do the *Field Work*, read the articles, and talk with some of the other teachers in my building about the kinds of things we are doing in our daily instruction" (*The LS Exchange*, Vol. 16, p. 3, 2003).

Most teachers strive to make unique and valuable contributions to session discussions by drawing on their own practical experience and insights. After dialoguing with colleagues, they leave each session with new ideas and an eagerness to improve their teaching practice. In between sessions, they engage in extension and reflection activities that help them apply new understandings to instruction.

As Keli again shares, "The information in the sessions along with the *Field Work* have given me new ideas and forced me to try new things in the classroom that can help my students learn and grow" (*The LS Exchange*, Vol. 6, p. 3, 2001). Her use of the term *forced* here is interesting because we know from our encounters with Keli and others that this is not meant to indicate that the professional development is coercive but rather to indicate that the professional development is compelling. Her ongoing professional learning experience, in other words, compels her to explore, adapt, and change her teaching practices.

Of course, each and every network member, whether field faculty, literacy specialist, or classroom teacher, does not meet these high expectations for professional development involvement all the time. For example, 100% attendance is not always the case for all meetings across the network, and not all teachers are eager learners and active participants in the professional development. In meeting some of these high expectations some of the time and in some measure, however, teachers create an energy that moves the professional development forward toward a fuller, richer learning experience for everyone involved. Each group within the network system, then, becomes a strong center for collaboration, interaction, shared meaning, and learning around the essential understandings of the core curriculum that frames the LS Project.

Still, the triadic groups within the network system cannot remain islands entirely unto themselves, each sharing and communicating only within their own boundaries. They must interconnect to bring new information to one another, to provide feedback to one another, and to share insights about what practices are making a difference in classroom reading instruction. Probably the most powerful bridge-builder between the groups is the literacy specialist who works with a field faculty member, other literacy specialists, and classroom teachers. As literacy specialists move from learners in the field faculty session to teachers of teachers in the professional development sessions, they bring fresh ideas and engaging activities to help teachers gain more knowledge and develop more skillful teaching practice. After they have taught a core curriculum session to the teachers, literacy specialists gather feedback and reflect on what seemed

LITERACY SPECIALIST MEETING AGENDA
January 7, 2004
9:00 AM TO 3:00 PM

Welcome and overview of agenda

Preview of new books and videos available to use in sessions

Housekeeping chores - paperwork & session dates

Introduction to Session 4

Lunch

Introduction to Session 5

Discussion of supplemental readings

Review of site visit procedures

Closing comments and questions

FIGURE 3.6. Field faculty–literacy specialist meeting agenda.

to work well and what seemed to work not so well, and what they need to change. At the next field faculty meeting, literacy specialists share their experiences and assist one another in planning ways to hone the next session. As literacy specialists continually engage in this teaching–learning cycle, they "feed forward" theories and research on effective reading and writing instruction and "feed back" teachers' realizations, struggles, and successes as they assist the teachers in gaining a deeper understanding of literacy content and pedagogy. In an interview following her field faculty member's observation of her sessions, a literacy specialist describes her thoughts about the process:

It confirms what I have been trying to accomplish this year and what I have done in the past several years. It makes me stronger in my background information because I'm presenting it to others. I feel a real responsibility to get it right, because these teachers are asking me questions. I need to be sure of terms and information that I'm presenting. As far as collegiality, it's really tied us together. We have common background knowledge and we can share and really know what each other's thinking about certain parts of literacy.

We encourage and support communication in several other ways, none of which is extraordinary or unusual in multilayered projects, but nonetheless effective. One of these is the distribution of a quarterly newsletter, *The LS Exchange*, which reports on network activities and features articles from the field faculty, literacy specialist, and classroom teacher perspectives.

Another effective communication tool is the traditional conference venue, where project participants learn new information together and also share highlights about their local successes. In our project, a spring conference is held regularly to provide this opportunity. Communication is apparent in our growing use of online tools for small-group consultations, e-learning courses, and the project website, where postings and exchanges, discussion groups, and project resources are available. (We discuss more about communication in the LS Project in Chapter 7.)

CLOSING

From our experience, a network system of organization works well in a large-scale implementation of a professional development curriculum because it supports small learning communities that are "wired together," so to speak, and also connected to larger project goals and activities. Our triadic network system forms small learning networks of classroom teachers, literacy specialists, and field faculty that break down geographic barriers and support differentiated levels of professional development. In brief, the network system puts professional learning groups within easy reach of one another, yet allows each to adapt to its local needs, thus building its own capacity for educator learning and change.

CHAPTER 4

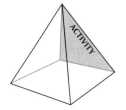

Implementation

Conducting a Professional Development Session with Literacy Specialists	Conducting a Professional Development Session with Classroom Teachers

An important goal of our teaching/coaching work is to share what we do and to learn from one another's experiences. Experience, as we all well know, is still the best teacher! How to make our experiences visible to one another, however, can be a bit of struggle.

—*The LS Exchange* (Vol. 2, p. 3, 2000)

In the first three chapters we described the LS Project in the abstract—its vision and foundations. In the next three chapters, we show you how the professional development model works at different levels of implementation. These chapters are filled with "slices of life" and particulars. How an actual session unfolds from preparing the literacy specialist to teach it to its delivery in schools is explained. We observe activities and processes in two different networks: field faculty led with literacy specialists and literacy specialist led with classroom teachers.

For this walk inside the learning networks, we focus on Session 1, which deals with the topic of literacy development—one of the components in the knowing domain explained in Chapter 2. We look closely at this opening session, which launches the professional development series, because it foregrounds the knowledge-building focus of the LS Project and features the project's three tenets in action at different levels of implementation. By the end of this chapter, you should have a better sense of how the intangibles of the LS Project become realized in the real-time interactions of its participants.

Before we join two different networks in progress, a few pieces of information are relevant. Session leaders, whether field faculty members or literacy specialists, prepare for their roles by previewing the session materials that support professional development. In preparation for the literacy specialist meeting, field faculty member Penny Freppon studied the background reading for Session 1, Knowing about Literacy Development, and also discussed it with other field faculty members at a prior monthly meeting. She also studied the before–during–after and extension activities described in the Session 1 folder.

Jill, one of the literacy specialists in Penny's group, subsequently prepared for her role as instructional leader of her classroom teacher group. She studied the key concepts of literacy development addressed in Session 1 and reviewed a tentative instructional plan made with the literacy specialists during their training meeting. Taking into consideration the strengths and needs of her classroom teacher group, Jill organized the instructional materials and mapped out a time frame for implementing Session 1. (A detailed account of Jill's session is given later in this chapter.) Realizing that her teacher group is busy, she sent them a reminder about the upcoming session and a preview of what they would do together when they met for the session.

For training purposes, literacy specialists spend an entire day with their field faculty–literacy specialist group but they have about 3 hours (often at the end of the school day) with their classroom teacher groups. Professional development for classroom teachers, however, is carried forward into practice through extension activities, which are generally completed in the classroom, thereby increasing the opportunity for continual professional learning through these intentional theory-to-practice links. The literacy specialist, as an instructional leader, supports the *Field Work* and *Making Connections* activities in different ways, from suggesting job-related activities to intensive coaching on a specific technique or intervention.

A lot happens all at once in a session. Because we want you as readers to gain a good sense of what the professional development is like, we use a blend of narrative and text headings to illustrate what happens in the learning networks of the professional development model. The narrative, we hope, will not only enliven the reading, but also show how the networks are mutually supporting professional learning.

CONDUCTING A PROFESSIONAL DEVELOPMENT SESSION WITH LITERACY SPECIALISTS

On a steamy, late summer day in southeastern Ohio, Penny Freppon, field faculty member, is meeting with her literacy specialist group. This is the first in a series of day-long sessions they will spend together over the next school year immersed in literacy content: studying, discussing, problem solving, and planning for effective instruction of the core curriculum. By the end of this day, Penny wants her 12 literacy specialists to leave confident in their knowledge of literacy development and well equipped to teach Session 1 of the core curriculum professional development series to their classroom teacher groups. We join her day at a point where the literacy specialists are considering the required readings for Session 1, and how they will help classroom teachers get the most out of these scientific articles. Each professional development session is accompanied by two or three research articles that explain theoretical frameworks and/or support specific teaching practices. All teachers are expected to read them for purposes of discussion and debate at each session (see supplemental readings list in Figure 4.1). We enter where Penny is engaged in some reflection-in-action about the articles for the first few sessions of the program and the literacy specialists' responses to them. Through her eyes, we then follow the course of activity to its end point: the literacy specialists' practical planning for Session 1 with their classroom teacher groups. As you observe through Penny's eyes, be alert to the structure that guides the professional development activity for literacy specialists: getting started, identifying potential problems, practicing, and making a plan.

Getting Started

In all honesty, I didn't think the literacy specialists would like the articles selected for the core curriculum's supplemental readings. The articles in the knowing domain are very challenging, especially the Charles Read piece on the linguistics of invented spelling [Read, 1971] and the Block on expert teaching [Block, Oakar, & Hurt, 2002]. However, I thought that the Session 1 articles on brain research and dyslexia [Shaywitz et al., 2000] and literacy development [Bear, 2001] would resonate with literacy specialists, and much to my delight, after voicing how dense (hard reading!) the articles were, the literacy specialists really got into discussing them. All the literacy specialists were interested, and I believe everyone in the room spoke up by asking a question or commenting. One literacy specialist was our critic. She had "bones to pick" with several statements in the articles. Having her speak out frequently was excellent, and she helped us "push" the idea of what we know now from research that we didn't know before we read the articles.

Identifying Potential Problems

Through discussion, the group found their way to an excellent set of questions: How can I teach this article to teachers? How can I help teachers interpret the material in meaningful ways? These questions emerged out of their

Session 1—Knowing about Literacy Development

Bear, D. (2001). "Learning to fasten the seat of my union suit without looking around": The synchrony of literacy development. *Theory into Practice, 30*, 149–157.

Shaywitz, B., Pugh, K., Jenner, A., Fulbright, R., Fletcher, J., Gore, J., & Shaywitz, S. (2000). The neurobiology of reading and reading disability (dyslexia). In M. Kamil, P. Mosenthal, P. D. Pearson, & R. Barr (Eds.), *Handbook of reading research* (Vol. 3, pp. 229–249). Mahwah, NJ: Erlbaum.

Session 2—Knowing about the English Language

Johnston, F. (2000). Spelling exceptions: Problems or possibilities? *The Reading Teacher, 54*, 372–378.

Read, C. (1971). Pre-school children's knowledge of English phonology. *Harvard Educational Review, 41*, 1–34.

Session 3—Knowing about Literacy Processes

Breznitz, A., & Berman, L. (2003). The underlying factors of word reading rate. *Educational Psychology Review, 15*, 247–265.

Stanovitch, K. (1994). Romance and reality. *The Reading Teacher, 47*, 280–291.

Session 4—Knowing about Literacy Education Models and Methods

Block, C., Oakar, M., & Hurt, N. (2002). The expertise of literacy teachers: A continuum from preschool to Grade 5. *Reading Research Quarterly, 37*, 178–206.

Lapp, D., & Flood, J. (1983). Approaches and methods of teaching reading: A historical view. In *Teaching reading to every child* (2nd ed., pp. 411–467). New York: Macmillan.

Session 5—Acknowledging Literacy Curriculum Expectations

Coburn, C. (2001). Collective sensemaking about reading: How teachers mediate reading policy in their professional communities. *Educational Evaluation and Policy Analysis, 23*, 145–170.

Darling-Hammond, L., & Falk, B. (1997). Using standards and assessments to support student learning. *Phi Delta Kappan, 79*, 190–199.

Session 6—Organizing Instruction

Henk, W., Moore, J., Marinak, B., & Tomasetti, B. (2000). A reading lesson observation framework for elementary teachers, principals, and literacy supervisors. *The Reading Teacher, 53*, 358–369.

Labov, W. (1995). Can reading failure be reversed: A linguistic approach to the question. In V. Gadsden & D. Wagner (Eds.), *Literacy among African-American youth: Issues in learning, teaching and schooling* (pp. 39–68). Cresskill, NJ: Hampton Press.

Session 7—Preparing the Literacy Environment

Labbo, L., & Kuhn, M. (2000). Weaving chains of affect and cognition: A young child's understanding of CD-ROM talking books. *Journal of Literacy Research, 32*, 187–210.

Smolin, L. I., & Lawless, K. A. (2003). Becoming literate in the technological age: New responsibilities and tools for teachers. *The Reading Teacher, 56*, 570–577.

Session 8—Bridging Home and School

Neuman, S., Caperelli, B., & Kee, C. (1998). Literacy learning, a family matter. *The Reading Teacher, 52*, 244–252.

Rogers, R. (2002). Between contexts: A critical discourse analysis of family literacy, discursive practices, and literate subjectivities. *Reading Research Quarterly, 37*, 248–277.

(continued)

FIGURE 4.1. Supplemental readings.

Session 9—Teaching Oral Language

Dickinson, D., McCabe, A., & Sprague, K. (2003). Teacher rating of oral language and literacy (TROLL): Individualizing early literacy instruction with a standards-based rating tool. *The Reading Teacher, 56*, 554–564.

Roth, F., Speece, D., & Cooper, D. (2002). A longitudinal analysis of the connection between oral language and early reading. *The Journal of Educational Research, 95*, 259–272.

Session 10—Teaching about Words

Beck, I., & McKeown, M. (2001). Text talk: Capturing the benefits of read-aloud experiences for young children. *The Reading Teacher, 55*, 10–20.

Penno, J., Wilkinson, A., & Moore, D. (2002). Vocabulary acquisition from teacher explanation and repeated listening to stories: Do they overcome the Matthew effect? *Journal of Educational Psychology, 94*, 23–33.

Session 11—Teaching Reading Comprehension

Pressley, M., & Wharton-McDonald, R. (1997). Skilled comprehension and its development through instruction. *School Psychology Review, 27*, 448–467.

Van den Branden, K. (2000). Does negotiation of meaning promote reading comprehension? A study of multilingual primary school classes. *Reading Research Quarterly, 35*, 426–433.

Session 12—Teaching Writing

Bradley, D. (2001). How beginning writers articulate and demonstrate their understanding of the act of writing. *Reading Research and Instruction, 40*, 273–296.

Staal, L. (2000). The story face: An adaptation of story mapping that incorporates visualization and discovery learning to enhance reading and writing. *The Reading Teacher, 54*, 27–31.

Session 13—Assessing Reading and Writing Behaviors

Ervin, R. (1998). Assessing early reading achievement: The road to results. *Phi Delta Kappan, 80*, 226–228.

Gillet, J. W., & Temple, C. (1994). Formal measures of reading ability. In C. Jennison (Ed.), *Understanding reading problems: Assessment and instruction* (4th ed., pp. 341–375). New York: HarperCollins College.

Session 14—Translating Assessment Results

Borko, H. (1997). New forms of classroom assessment: Implications for staff development. *Theory into Practice, 36*, 231–238.

Morris, D., Blanton, L., Blanton, W., & Perney, J. (1995). Spelling instrcution and achievement in six classrooms. *The Elementary School Journal, 96*(2), 145–162.

Session 15—Reflecting on Literacy Assessment Goals and Uses

Camilli, G., Vargas, S., & Yurecko, M. (2003). Teaching children to read: The fragile link between science and the federal education policy. *Education Policy Analysis Archives, 11*(15). Retrieved May 23, 2003, from http://epaa.asu.edu/epaa/v11n15/

International Reading Association. (2000). Excellent reading teachers: A position statement of the International Reading Association. *The Reading Teacher, 54*(2), 235–240.

Paris, S., & Carpenter, R. (2003). Center for the improvement of Early Reading Achievement: FAQs about IRIs. *The Reading Teacher, 56*, 578–580.

FIGURE 4.1. *(continued)*

discussion, and I was glad I could keep quiet long enough for things to unfold among them. The group was especially worried about teachers' responses to the brain article. They asked: Will teachers assume that if children have differently activated brains that there is nothing they can do about it? What instruction or intervention can help this problem? They also thought the invented spelling piece might prompt teachers to "skill and drill" students.

So we decided the best thing to do when working with these research articles with teachers was to make sure that no one walked away with any kind of misinterpretations that could lead to "misguided practices." Thus, in preparation for each article, we decided to (1) read for what we want teachers to walk away with, (2) what we don't want them to walk away with, and (3) to discuss these points in our meetings as well as what the articles have taught us. For each reading and follow-up discussion, we agreed on two purposes: to process (comprehend) the content of the articles, and to create ways to present and discuss the content with teachers.

We will pause here in this vignette for a few summary points about what is happening in this field faculty–literacy specialist learning group. The emphasis, as you can see, is on knowledge building through reading, discussing, and debating scientific articles that inform the topic at hand, literacy development. Penny's activity with the literacy specialists brings to life Tenet 1, *professional development expands and deepens knowledge of teaching and instruction*. The literacy specialists engage in tough deliberations about the content of the articles for a twofold reason: to understand it themselves and to prepare themselves to help their teacher groups understand it. They know the reading will be slow, but they also know that their teacher groups need to persevere in order to better understand the meaning of their own practice. Also significant is the literacy specialists' realization that misconceptions can result from a half-hearted reading of the articles, and so they develop a three-part strategy to handle this potential hazard in the teachers' professional development experience. They agree on what needs to be understood for more effective practice and what might be misunderstood, leading to misguided practices. On this point, we return to the session as Penny and colleagues practice techniques for engaging teachers with the content of the knowing domain articles and make their final plans for conducting Session 1 with classroom teacher groups.

Practicing

Jill, a literacy specialist and full-time reading teacher, led our discussion of the Stanovich article on the research people like and the research people don't like [Stanovich, 1994], which created quite a stir. She had everyone draw a slip of paper that had a question or comment taken from the article. (The page number of the article was included.) Next, the literacy specialists read their designated passage, talked with a partner briefly, and then joined in a whole-group discussion. This took time, but the conversations were most thoughtful. To conclude, Jill had all of us use a Venn diagram showing "things we like" and "things we didn't like." For example, in one circle of the Venn diagram were listed things we appreciated in the Stanovich article; the other circle listed some things we didn't like in his article [see Figure 4.2]. Where the circles of the Venn diagram intersected we listed middle-ground ideas and practices we agreed upon. The literacy specialists enjoyed this reading technique and we all decided we'd find new techniques to use for future readings as we discussed them in our meetings.

The discussion of the article by Cathy Collins Block on expert teaching [Block et al., 2002], led by Karen, another literacy specialist, was a hit. Everyone resonated and connected with it. The literacy specialists thought it would be easy to read with their teachers (with help to understand the research method as needed). Although the literacy specialists didn't talk much about methods of research in this session, our "critic" raised good questions about method with regard to control for confounding variables. We also saw Block's article as an important piece for administrators to read.

Jina, another literacy specialist, led the discussion of the Charles Read linguistic-grounded invented spelling article [Read, 1971]. Jina told us about her strategies to best understand this dense article. Jina reread the article and she used a small mirror to "glide" her tongue and make other mouth move-

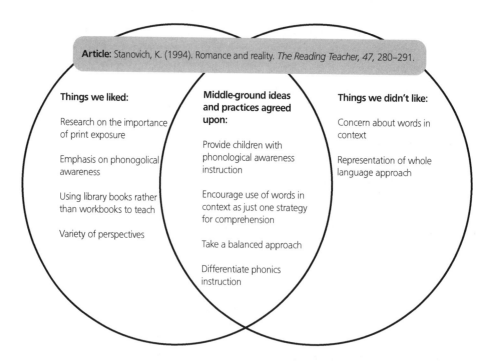

FIGURE 4.2. Venn diagram illustrating article discussion points.

ments as she pronounced so she could physically feel and see the kinds of things Read discussed. This insight helped all of us, and soon we were practicing gliding our tongues and pronouncing /jragon/ for dragon to see, hear, and feel the sounds in our mouths as children do when they spell inventively. We decided two things. One is that young children are brilliant in making sense of the English spelling system, and the other is that it's a good idea to have teachers bring a small mirror to the session as a hands-on strategy to help teachers interact with the Read article. We also thought that teachers should bring in their children's writing samples to compare and contrast with the points in this article and to consider how infants and very young children learn as they put nearly everything, it seems, in their mouths.

I took on Shaywitz's article (Shaywitz et al., 2000) and did a K–W–L [Ogle, 1986] adaptation. Each literacy specialist did her own K–W–L, and I did mine. We walked through the procedures and talked. I also had two overheads that showed slices of an fMRI brain image. With these images I could point out what a few of the brain areas mentioned in the article looked like and where they were located. I went last and folks were tired. The K–W–L did not get completed, but I think it helped and we could see how the K–W–L would be a helpful strategy to use with teachers. Bonnie, another literacy specialist, brought an article from *The Wall Street Journal* on brain research to add to our reading on the topic. With Bonnie's help, we talked further and learned more about the brain as it relates to literacy learning.

Making a Plan

The literacy specialists immediately saw the usefulness of techniques, such as the K–W–L and the Venn diagram, to facilitate substantive dialogue about the content of the articles among their teacher groups. They also agreed that having discussion leaders for each article worked well. The organizing questions—What do I want teachers to walk away with from this article? And how shall I make sure that the concepts in the readings are not misinterpreted?—helped them prepare for the uncertainties of discussion with teacher groups and guide their responses when conversations might get confused or off track. To close the loop on this aspect of planning the professional development session they would implement with the teachers, the literacy specialists added the question: How can I relate this (article content) to instruction? This practical question propelled them to think ahead to how these new ideas can break through the realities of classroom instruction.

They then turned their attention to the immediate planning steps associated with the Session 1 folder. For this, they first previewed the folder. Then I led them through the before–during–after segments of the session before they outlined their plan for implementing each part.

At this point, we step away from this field faculty-led session as it addresses the particulars of presenting the session to teachers. Before leaving it entirely, though, we wish to underscore a few key ideas. Taking time, as Penny did, with "tough-to-get-through" articles is so important because it deepens the literacy specialists' knowledge base and at the same time prepares them for doing the same with their teacher groups.

How this was accomplished is equally as important as the content examined. First we note the emphasis on learning with understanding, bringing to bear preexisting experiences and encouraging active engagement with conceptually difficult content, which the literacy specialists must strive to represent in their own instructional settings. They, like Penny, need to create a stimulating, yet safe, place for professional learning that ensures teachers will know more when they are done than when they began the session, and that this new information can be carried forward to the classroom setting.

Next, we note the focus on critical discussion among colleagues—making public one's views and concerns—that develops a stance of critique and inquiry toward practice and builds individual reflective abilities (Ball & Cohen, 1999). Participants are asked to express ideas, to query, to challenge, and to disagree, thus creating a climate for debate and a place to deliberate. These intellectually charged discourse processes can build collaborative relationships between educators as they learn to appreciate one another's experiences, thinking, problem solving, intelligence, and leadership. Cultivating these cognitive and social processes in the course of preparing the literacy specialists for their role as professional developers reflects relationship building, which literacy specialists also need to apply in their work. Collaborative relationships contribute mightily to the significance and priority individuals give to new ideas and information. Their strength can help convince teachers that an idea is worth considering, that it might be useful, that it can be challenged, and that it can be adapted to one's own instructional context.

CONDUCTING A PROFESSIONAL DEVELOPMENT SESSION WITH CLASSROOM TEACHERS

We now turn to following Jill from the all-day meeting with Penny and colleagues to her own local school district. Here she will present Session 1 on the topic of literacy development to 15 primary-grade teachers who teach together in a rural, midwestern elementary school. It is just before 3:30 P.M. when the session begins, and we join her as she mentally ticks through what she has done to prepare for it. Since it is Session 1, she is a bit nervous, but she feels well prepared and confident that her peers will find the time spent worthwhile.

Your brief time with Jill will help you gain a sense of how a session goes and also reveal the underlying structure that supports each and every professional development session with teachers. Toward the end of this abbreviated session, you will see real evidence of how the literacy specialist and classroom teacher networks overlap and stay true to the professional learning goals of the professional development program. We begin the vignette with Jill's thoughts about how she planned for her session and then take you inside her session where we expose the before–during–after structure and the learning activities that typify professional development in the LS Project.

Presession Preparation

I'm glad I took enough time to review notes from the articles on literacy development and revisit the plan we developed together at the literacy specialists meeting with Penny a few days ago, because I had to make a few last-minute time adjustments. I feel better prepared to answer questions that may arise in discussions after reading chapters from *How People Learn: Brain, Mind, Experience, and School* [Bransford et al., 2000] and *Much More Than the ABCs* [Schickedanz, 1999], two of the five reference books listed in the Session 1 folder.

I know it will be more meaningful to use local samples of student work, and I have those ready to use in place of those provided in the session folder. Let's see . . . I've got my copy of *Ohio Academic Content Standards K–12 English Language Arts* and the transparencies, activity packet, and *Field Work* procedures are right here. Good . . .

Inside the Session

With the folder for Session 1 in hand, Jill enters the meeting with her teacher group shortly before 3:30 P.M. They will work together until slightly past 6:00 P.M. We narrate her enactment of the before–during–after framework or simply the BDA. You may recognize the BDA as that familiar structure we expect to see in a well-crafted reading lesson. For the purpose of illustrating how this structure sets up a learning context in a professional development session, the parts of the BDA are: *Before* (Share, Introduce, Explain/Show), *During* (Organize, Do, Record), and *After* (Present, Discuss, Summarize). (See Chapter 2 for further explanation of the session framework.)

Before: Tapping Experience and Introducing New Concepts

Share. Since this is the first session of the school year, Jill begins with a review of the overall core curriculum content and the BDA format that frames each session. She asks each teacher to share one idea about what he or she expects to gain from participating in the professional development series.

Introduce. After stating the topic of the session, Knowing About Literacy Development, she reads the children's picture book *Leo the Late Bloomer* written by Robert Kraus (1971). All join in as they discuss the critical idea of variation in children's development. Jill draws the teachers' attention to the Professional Learning Goals for this session (Figure 4.3) and invites the teachers to personalize them. She records their ideas on chart paper and posts it as a quick reference for keeping the session focused.

Jill then discusses the importance of having a shared vocabulary for professional development and begins a word wall on a portable bulletin board, which she brings to all sessions. The group brainstorms what they think the terms *continuum*, *development*, *literacy*, and *language* mean, and then teachers check their definitions with those provided on the Session 1 folder. Jill posts these terms on the bulletin board.

Next, she engages the teachers in a K–W–L about literacy development. They discuss the importance of activating prior knowledge in new learning situations, noting how this activity piques their interest in the topic just as the strategy will pique students' interest in a topic—any topic.

Explain/Show. To move into this phase of the session, Jill presents overhead transparencies of the literacy development continuum. She asks teachers to compare the characteristics listed on the continuum with their ideas listed on the K–W–L chart. Comparing and contrasting, they add new information about reading and writing development to their own K–W–L charts.

She then focuses their attention on a transcription of a first-grade child's record of oral reading. She explains the notations for the miscues and mimics reading how the child may have read the passage, with substitutions, omissions, erratic pausing, and word-by-word reading. After reading, Jill guides the teachers' analysis by asking questions that provoke critical thinking (Figure 4.4) and interpretations that are grounded in the observational data noted on the oral reading record.

Explain the continuums of talking, reading, writing, and spelling development.

Interpret individual children's phases of development from observational data.

Apply understanding of development to literacy instruction.

Reflect on application of developmental continuums to planning literacy instruction.

FIGURE 4.3. Professional learning goals for Session 1, Knowing about Literacy Development.

What Will Little Bear Wear? From *Little Bear* by Elsa Minarik (1957) [82 Words] Harper Trophy

It is cold.
See the snow.

       came
See the snow come down.   substitution

 brother
Little Bear said, "Mother Bear,   substitution
I am cold.
See the snow.

s/c.   *something*
went   */sum-th-ing/*
I want something to put on."   substituted *went* for <u>want</u> and self-corrected;
                                sounded out <u>something</u>

So Mother Bear made something.   word-by-word reading
for Little Bear.   word-by-word reading

"See, Little Bear," she /// said,   pausing 3 seconds before <u>said</u>
"I have ///something for my little bear. pausing 3 seconds before something; said <u>little</u>
Here it is.   in syllables
Put it on your head,"   word-by-word reading

"Oh," said Little Bear,
"it is a hat.

ohhhh
Hurray! Now I will not be cold."   substituted *ohhhh* for <u>hurray</u>; used expression
Little Bear went (out) to play.   omitted <u>out</u>

Jill: What do we observe?

Teacher: Justin's oral reading record shows that he made five miscues in reading the words the first time through and self-corrected one of them.

Teacher: His errors are primarily substitutions with words that graphically resemble the text.

Teacher: He delayed in saying the words <u>said</u> and <u>something</u> about midway through reading the passage and omitted the word <u>out</u> from the last sentence, which somewhat alters the meaning of the text.

Jill: What about his use of decoding skills?

Teacher: He shows some use of decoding skills in sounding out two-syllable words, <u>something</u> and <u>little</u>. Other substitutions, <u>came</u> and <u>brother</u>, he did not self-correct.

Jill: Yes, while both are syntactically acceptable, they do alter the meaning of the text. Justin read in mostly a word-by-word, monotone voice. He read the last line with expression. Do you see how to figure his accuracy? Who has a calculator?

Teacher: I do. I'll plug in the numbers when you tell me.

Jill: Take 82 words, subtract the 4 miscues. This equals 78 words correct. (*to the teacher with the calculator*) Divide by 82 total words. What do you get?

Teacher: 95%.

FIGURE 4.4. Sample first grader's record of oral reading and conversation to guide observation.

They pause at this point and Jill asks a hard question: *Now that we have analyzed this record, what does it mean?* The teachers are not so forthcoming with their responses, so Jill directs them to the reading developmental continuum. After considering this information, they decide that Justin's reading behaviors are characteristic of a beginning reader. He is heavily focused on decoding the words and he is not yet fluent. He uses letter–sound knowledge to figure out unfamiliar words and is able to recognize consonant–vowel–consonant patterns in longer words (e.g., *lit* in *little*), and smaller words within longer words (e.g., *some* in *something*). They conclude that the text is at an appropriate level for instruction, which was based on calculating the percentage of accurate reading at 95%, although the reading was neither smooth nor prosodic.

To pin this analysis to classroom instruction, Jill asks the teachers to identify teaching techniques that will pull Justin's literacy development forward. Among others, they suggest fluency strategies, such as repeated reading in familiar text and partner reading. Jill interjects that they will also need to monitor his progress toward the benchmark of at least 60 words correct per minute by the end of first grade. She stretches the teachers' thinking by explaining that Justin needs to be read to in text more difficult than he himself can read, that he needs frequent exposure to the syntactic and semantic features of more complex text, and that he needs to listen to the teacher's modeling of fluent reading.

Using a similar approach, Jill involves the group in analyzing a writing sample. After comparing the characteristics of the composition to the writing development continuum, she goes one step further. She asks the teachers to make connections between what the student knows and needs to learn. The teachers describe the student's writing performance in relation to English language arts standards, noting strengths and weaknesses.

During: Engaging in Collaborative Problem Solving

Organize. Following whole-group instruction, which taps and builds background knowledge on the topic, Jill has the teachers form small groups for purposes of collaborative problem solving. In this session, the small groups have two tasks: to examine a set of oral language, reading, writing, and spelling samples; and to identify what the students know and need to learn to advance as readers and writers and to meet the state benchmarks for student achievement.

Do. Jill distributes the samples of oral language, oral reading, and writing that she collected from their classrooms the week before the session, along with the report template for documenting their work. She decided to use student samples from the teachers' classrooms rather than those provided with the session materials. She figured that their own local samples would be more relevant and meaningful to them and also help them see the immediate value of continuing on with the same kind of collaborative inquiry beyond the professional development session context.

As the teachers examine and discuss the samples, Jill checks in on their progress. She observes that there is much talk and the tasks keep the groups engaged. They want to know if they are right. She reminds them that they are looking for patterns in growth or development, not right answers.

Record. After the small groups work for about 40 minutes, Jill tells them to finalize their written comments and prepare to summarize their findings.

After: Organizing and Extending New Ideas and Concepts

Present. Jill asks each group to present its findings and build on the previous group's presentation as they explain their analyses.

Discuss. The presentations lead to a comparison of teachers' observations to the developmental continuum generated earlier. Jill observes that they feel confident in their knowledge and ability. To her question, *Why use a developmental continuum?*, they respond by discussing several rationales. She links the teachers' rationales to their personal professional goals for the school year: *What do we want our students to be like as readers and writers when they leave us at the end of this year?* She also underscores the idea, *We need to look at what children can do and to use our understanding of development to know where we want to lead them next.*

Summarize. Jill reviews the teachers' ideas and questions about literacy development they listed on the K–W–L chart at the beginning of the session, to which she records new information and insights that they reported in their whole-group discussion. She emphasizes how effective reading instruction takes into account students' reading and writing development, systematic observations of individual reading and writing behaviors, and learning expectations as defined by the state English language arts standards. She transitions from this portion of the session to the reflection segment by reading the book *Wolf!* (Bloom, 1999), which prompts a short but lively discussion.

Before closing with a reflection on the learning experience, Jill steps out of the immediate mode of what they will do next to draw the teachers' attention to the organization of the session. She pulls them into metacognitive thinking about the BDA structure and helps them see the parallels to a well-designed reading lesson design. Each professional development session has processes that teachers engage in as learners. With the assistance of a knowledgeable and skillful literacy specialist, the teachers can be brought to heightened awareness about the learning activities that they plan and implement with their own students.

Reflection. After they discuss the BDA and its application to their own practice, Jill draws attention to one of the professional learning goals: reflection on new learning. Last but not least, she gives the teachers a few minutes to think back on the sessions and respond to one of the reflection prompts (Figure 4.5) in a personal log or journal. She distributes journals for recording their reflections about this session and the upcoming ones, and then invites the teachers to record their reflections on what they have learned and how they will apply this learning to their own practice.

What's Next?

Session 1 learning does not end with the end of the session for Jill nor for her teacher group. Before they leave, Jill explains the extension activities that stretch opportunities for professional learning beyond the session itself. Their purpose is twofold: to extend the teachers' understanding of the session content into the classroom and to reinforce and enrich the content through reading and discussion.

Jill reviews the *Field Work* and *Making Connections* activities for Session 1 and reminds teachers that the results will be shared and discussed with other teachers at the next session. She points out how the *Field Work* requires them to apply new concepts and skills to their own school and classroom. She stresses their value for practicing higher level teaching and thinking skills in the classroom, such as analyzing student work for evidence of literacy development and gearing instruction to it.

Next, Jill describes the research-based articles that accompany Session 1. And, as you have probably figured out, we are now at that point where we began with Penny and her literacy specialists: grappling with those scientific articles on literacy development. Now these articles will serve as a follow-up activity that reinforces the content of Session 1 and a point of departure for the upcoming

---

Take a moment to reflect about this session.
Respond to the following prompts in your log or journal.

Summary: a brief description of the key points
New Learning: major new insights that come out of the session for you
Questions: questions that emerge from topics, issues, or strategies
Personal: a personal reaction to the context, content, or strategies used

SUMMARY → NEW LEARNING → QUESTIONS → PERSONAL REACTION

FIGURE 4.5. Sample of reflection prompts for the core curriculum sessions.

Session 2. Jill has selected two out of the four articles for the teachers to read before the next session.

She asks for teacher leaders who will facilitate the discussion of each article during the sharing part of the next session; she suggests techniques they can use to guide their fellow teachers in the discussion of each article (e.g., question starters, as Jill demonstrated, or the K–W–L that Penny used). Jill explains that these extension activities are intended to help the teachers retain, review, consider, and actually begin to apply the content on literacy development that they are learning in the session to their own practice. These activities are meaningful ways to reinforce and enrich their knowledge through reading and discussion.

As the teachers prepare to leave the session, Jill checks attendance sheets and thinks about her presentation of materials and the teachers' responses to the activities. She records her observations, thoughts, ideas, and interpretations of the session in her journal:

> Everything went very well. I was pleased with the teachers' comments following the session. I'm glad I made changes to the format to add my own creativity because of the knowledge I have of the teaching staff. The content of this session proved valuable for all teachers as they started out the school year. Knowing the culture of the professional community helps me provide meaningful learning experiences that the teachers will take away and apply to their own practice.

Walking away from this session, we hold several of its salient features in mind. Although there are other features worth commenting on, these stand out for us. First, it is evident that Jill planned carefully for the professional session, taking into account the interests, preferences, and concerns of her colleagues. She adapted some parts to make them more relevant to the teachers (e.g., she used their student work samples instead of the ones provided in the session folder). She also embedded interesting activities to stimulate the teachers' interest. Second, she deliberately modeled the BDA instructional framework and later pointed this out to the teachers, using it as an example of how to organize instruction to enhance learning. Third, she steadily built on what the teachers already knew and worked to deepen their knowledge during all phases of the lesson. She drew out what they knew and used this to build their confidence and to link new ideas with those already in place. And fourth, she encouraged substantive conversation (on the complex topic of literacy development) and personal involvement (sharing of experience) to create a sense of belonging and shared professional learning among colleagues. These are important to highlight because they show the three guiding tenets of professional development at work in the local professional development setting, namely, evidence of effort to deepen and extend teachers' knowledge, to create favorable conditions for their learning, and to build relationships that motivate and inspire them to return for more.

Acknowledging the tremendous variability in professional development activity, we also see commonalities in its process and structure, and we invite you to consider these with us. Professional development is a process of meaning making through interaction and involvement with content and with others. Strengthening that process entails careful consideration of adult learners, the content to be learned, and the authenticity of activities for learning. Coordinating these three elements in a sociocultural context is demanding. It requires considerable deliberation and forethought. Simultaneously, professional development needs structured activity that supports change in teaching skills over time. Here the BDA structure is especially useful. It offers three interrelated microperiods for change to occur, starting with what the teacher knows (before) to interactions (during and after) that stimulate changes in teacher knowledge and skill.

CLOSING

We bring to a close our brief look inside networks with a few final points. Professional development, like all of human learning, is complex. It contains a tremendous amount of variability among participants, the material resources, the context, and the activity itself. Consequently, it is not possible to adequately show completely what professional development is in the LS Project or to represent its reality within and across networks. In this chapter, we offered a glimpse of what professional development looks like as it happened in two network settings, but it is a thin strip of reality. Consider this as you integrate this descriptive information into your experience. There is, in other words, more to the story.

We have included in Appendices A and B two vignettes that follow the planning and delivering of professional development through the eyes of literacy specialists. These vignettes emphasize the unique nature of the professional development within the network and a variety of school settings.

In the next chapter, we follow the course of professional development from the session into the classroom setting where teachers read and reflect more, and complete the extension activities *Field Work* and *Making Connections*. Coaching in the sense of working individually with teachers provides additional support to some teachers and links professional learning goals to professional development and raises the bar on applying new learning to practice. Extending the reach of the session content into the classroom helps to make the professional development significant and productive as literacy specialist and teachers interact within the classroom setting.

CHAPTER 5

Professional Development into Practice

| What Are Extensions? | Why Are Extensions Important? | How Do Extensions Support Practice? |

I am overwhelmed by the excitement of the teachers that I am working with. I am seeing and hearing evidence of the success of the core curriculum on a daily basis. Teachers are sharing ideas and showing how things are working in their classrooms. In the classrooms I am noticing that teachers are utilizing strategies that have been discussed and they are showing a confident understanding of new learning.

—*The LS Exchange* (Vol. 7, p. 7, 2001)

An essential component of effective professional development is the *follow-through*, the thinking, the activity, and the conversations that bridge learning in the professional development setting to everyday practice. Many session activities, such as discussing the latest literacy research, interpreting video lessons, and analyzing samples of oral reading records, provide valuable learning experiences and provoke deeper thinking about practice. To bring the conceptual content of these activities closer to everyday practice, teachers need to be collecting and analyzing data on their own students. They need to be planning, teaching, and reflecting on their own instruction (Ball & Cohen, 1999; Gallimore & Goldenberg, 2001; National Staff Development Council, 2001; Schon, 1987). This is indeed the bridge between abstract understandings gained in the professional development session and their application in individual classroom practice. In other words, teachers need many opportunities to localize their learning and to intersect new ideas and strategies with their existing practice. In the LS Project, teachers follow through by applying concepts in the less certain world of the real school and classroom. To further develop their learning network, many teachers choose to work with other teachers or their literacy specialist in carrying out these activities.

We ended our last chapter with a close look at what occurs *inside* a structured, 3-hour professional development session. Recall that the literacy specialist leads teachers in sharing theoretical ideas, examining new content, modeling strategies, and critically analyzing problems of practice related to the concepts and skills studied during the session. We described how the literacy specialist ends each session by explaining the activities that teachers will do *outside* the session to extend their learning.

In this chapter, we describe two kinds of extension activities: *Field Work* and *Making Connections*. As shown in Figure 5.1, these extensions are designed to bridge learning in the professional development session to the more immediate contexts of district, school, classroom, and community. First we define these extensions, describe them, and explain why they are important. Then, we provide examples to illustrate how extension activities are used to (1) support schoolwide change, (2) develop home–school relationships, and (3) improve reading and writing instruction. When reading these examples of *Field Work* and *Making Connections* activities, note how they are interwoven when applied in school settings. This calls for close reading to envision their critical role as bridge builders in the LS Project.

WHAT ARE EXTENSIONS?

Field Work is a structured activity that situates the concepts and strategies teachers encounter in the session and allows them to flexibly manipulate these ideas in their own school setting. Our use of the term *field work* is intentional. It communicates that the activity is professional work integral to skilled teaching. In carrying out the *Field Work* activity, teachers apply understandings toward the goal of improving their practice. Field work is not busy work. It is carefully designed to extend learning from group sessions to individual settings.

Field Work is a classroom application that parallels the problem-solving activity carried out during the session. During Session 1, Knowing about Literacy Development, for example, the literacy specialist guides teachers in analyzing students' writing samples to identify features that demonstrate a continuum of spelling development. The teachers have ample time to study different samples on their own or in small groups, with the literacy specialist there to assist with analysis and to prompt discussion.

Field Work

PURPOSE: To examine literacy samples from a developmental perspective to determine what students know and need to learn (FW1.1).

DIRECTIONS

Collect oral language, reading, and writing samples from one student.

Study the samples from a developmental perspective and record observations.

Identify the appropriate Standard and Grade-level Indicators that most closely align with what the student knows and needs to learn.

Choose one area of need and design an instructional strategy to enhance the student's literacy development.

Record your analysis on the chart and outline an instructional strategy on the reverse side.

Observations of literacy characteristics:	Use the samples to identify appropriate Standard and Grade-level Indicators that most closely align with what the student knows and needs to learn. Grade Level_____
Oral Language	Standard:
	Indicator(s):
Reading	Standard:
	Indicator(s):
Writing	Standard:
	Indicator(s):
Spelling	Standard:
	Indicator(s):

MAKING CONNECTIONS

You have been invited to make a presentation on literacy development at a district-wide parent meeting. Provide an outline of the main points of your talk.

COMING UP

Next session:
KNOWING ABOUT THE ENGLISH LANGUAGE

• Explore three basic elements of the English language as a writing system.

• Interpret how these basic elements characterize written English.

• Reflect on the importance of knowing the English language on early literacy instruction.

FIGURE 5.1. Panel 5 of the five-panel core curriculum session folder.

Some time between that group session and the next one, teachers carry out *Field Work* by collecting samples of reading, writing, and oral language from different students in their classrooms. The literacy specialist provides a set of procedures and an activity worksheet for teachers to record their observations, analyses, and reflections on their students' samples. Based on their analyses, they draw inferences about literacy development to determine what students already know and need to learn to advance toward reading and writing proficiency. The teachers bring the student work samples and their analyses and interpretations to the next session to share their findings and teaching ideas.

Making Connections, like *Field Work*, provides relevant and meaningful learning experiences linked to practice. Less structured in design than *Field Work*, *Making Connections* presents scenarios or opportunities of practice to further link teachers' understandings developed in the professional development sessions to the broader concerns of their schools and communities. Developing a presentation for parents on the role of oral language in literacy development, for example, requires teachers to use their knowledge in creative, engaging ways to decide what and how to communicate to a parent audience. *Making Connections* also demands critical thinking by setting up situations that require teachers to conduct inquiries, such as reexamining their local report card to see how well it aligns with learning expectations. As literacy specialist Nancy describes:

> After the discussion of the development of literacy [Session 1], they [teachers] were critical of the local report card for grades kindergarten through three. For example, on the second-grade report card, the teachers noticed that the heading was oral and written language. However, there was nothing listed for oral communication. Another problem: If a child is developmentally advanced for his grade level, there is no place to show his abilities at his level. (*The LS Exchange*, Vol. 3, p. 5, 2000)

Additionally, *Making Connections* also sets up situations for teachers to explain aspects of their teaching work to other colleagues, parents, and stakeholders by creating displays of instruction, preparing presentations for a school board meeting (e.g., how standards are embedded in daily lessons), or interpreting the results of schoolwide data from reading assessments.

WHY ARE EXTENSIONS IMPORTANT?

Based on our tenets, *Field Work* and *Making Connections* press teachers to extend their learning about literacy content and pedagogy. We observe how professional development expands and deepens educators' knowledge, as teachers think critically and reflectively about their own classroom settings and think more broadly about the educational contexts of home, school, district, and community (Tenet 1). We find evidence that professional development creates favorable conditions for learning when teachers draw on their prior knowledge and experience as they apply new ideas in a supportive learning environment with their colleagues (Tenet 2). We see how extensions guide professional development that builds human relationships, creating opportunities for peer collaboration and for literacy specialists to work alongside teachers, assisting them toward more skillful practice (Tenet 3).

Extension activities are considered to be integral components of each professional development session and need to be meaningful so that the teachers will be motivated to do them, recognizing their relevance for improving teaching in ways that will improve student performance. At the end of each session, the literacy specialist spends 10–15 minutes explaining the *Field Work* purpose, procedures, and activity pages and introducing the *Making Connections* scenarios. Teachers then carry out the activity in the weeks between the sessions and bring their artifacts and reflections to share as a springboard for the next session. In other words, the extension activities serve to connect learning in the professional development session to learning in everyday teaching work. The bridging of professional development learning contexts and everyday practice is captured in Figure 5.2.

HOW DO EXTENSIONS SUPPORT PRACTICE?

We continue with three examples of extensions. The first focuses on schoolwide change from Session 5. The second focuses on home–school relationships from Session 8. The third focuses on the literacy learning environment from Session 7. These descriptions of different kinds of *Field Work* and *Making Connections* expose the links between the concepts and skills explored in the group session and the extensions to practice. We want our readers to focus on how the *Field*

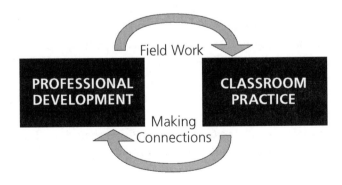

Learning in Professional Development Sessions and Learning in Practice

FIGURE 5.2. Bridging learning contexts.

Work activity flows directly from the problem-solving segment of the session and also sets up a coaching context for the literacy specialist and teachers to collaborate in sharpening instructional practices.

Extensions That Support Schoolwide Change

For professional development to contribute to schoolwide reform, it is important that teachers have ample opportunity to critically examine factors in the larger school community and note how they may impede or support the achievement of desired educational goals. Issues surrounding standards, assessment, core reading programs, report cards, and accountability are prevalent in today's school communities. Large and small districts face many challenges in resolving these issues to reach the goal of academic and social success for all students. Although integral to a larger system, individual schools have their own specific populations to serve and unique strategies they deem appropriate for helping them achieve high academic and social outcomes. Likewise, the classroom teacher, also integral to the larger system, has a responsibility for putting into place the structures, routines, and activities that assure success for all students.

Example of Field Work

Session 5, Acknowledging Literacy Curriculum Expectations, examines the Ohio English language arts standards and specific grade-level indicators. During the whole group discussion of the topic during the session, teachers use the lens of what students should know and be able to do to consider what teachers need to know and be able to do so that students will achieve success. An analytic guide as shown in Figure 5.3 provides a structure for teachers to review the standards and record questions related to each domain of practice: knowing, planning, teaching, and assessing. Their discussion deepens as teachers respond to the questions and begin to self-assess their knowledge and skills.

This discussion is followed by a problem-solving activity that involves analyzing video clips of a writing lesson. The literacy specialist leads a discussion of the lesson plan prior to viewing the video and motivates the teachers to watch by asking them to predict what they would expect to see in the lesson.

Next, the teachers work in small groups to observe the video lesson and respond to several questions. Some questions are designed to sharpen observation skills by directing teachers to note specific teaching actions and teacher–student interactions. Others are designed to provoke critical thinking about the instruction—for example, whether or not it is geared to the student with particular needs, how to adapt the instruction to different learners, how they would apply the teaching strategy to their own instruction.

Following session activities and discussions, teachers are introduced to a *Field Work* activity designed to extend learning. Session 5 *Field Work* engages

Ohio Academic Content Standards: K–12 English Language Arts Writing Process Benchmarks (Ohio Dept. of Education, 2002) Benchmarks are what students are expected to know and be able to do by the end of grade level band (e.g., third grade)	Teachers' Knowledge and Skills Within a standards-based teaching framework, teachers ask themselves what they need to know and be able to do to assist students in achieving the benchmarks.			
	KNOWING	**PLANNING**	**TEACHING**	**ASSESSING**
A. Generate ideas for written compositions.	What do I need to know about writing?	How should I organize writing instruction?	What are some effective strategies for teaching writing?	What are ways to assess writing?
B. Develop audience and purpose for self-selected and assigned writing tasks.				How do I anaylze students' writing samples?
C. Using organizers to clarify ideas for writing assignments.	What are writing expectations for different age groups?	How do I select writing prompts?	What are effective prewriting teaching strategies?	
D. Use revision strategies and resources to improve ideas and content, organization, word choice and detail.	What is the writing process?	Where can I find effective graphic organizers?	How do I scaffold writing instruction?	How do I measure students' progress in writing?
E. Edit to improve sentence fluency, grammar and usage.	What are the writing conventions and proper grammatical structures?	How will I set-up a writing center?		How do I involve students in self-assessment of their writing?
F. Apply tools to judge the quality of writing.			How can I motivate students to write?	
G. Publish writing samples for display or sharing with others using techniques, such as electronic resources and graphics.				

FIGURE 5.3. Using standards to self-assess knowledge and skills for teaching writing effectively.

teachers in the planning and implementation of a standards-based lesson. The following *Field Work* procedures guide the teachers through the planning process:

- Specify the instructional focus (e.g., oral language, phonemic awareness, comprehension, fluency, vocabulary, writing).
- Identify the standard.
- Describe the lesson.
- List the materials.
- Name specific actions to carry out before, during, and after the lesson.
- Describe how the students will be assessed.
- Explain how the lesson will be critiqued.

TEACHING ENGLISH LANGUAGE ARTS
LESSON PLAN TEMPLATE

English Language Arts Standard:
Phonemic Awareness, Word Recognition, and Fluency

Grade-Level Indicator(s):
Kindergarten—Identify and complete rhyming words and patterns

Focus of Instruction:
Students will participate in the shared reading of a rhyming book, recognize rhyming words, and create their own silly rhymes.

Description of Lesson:
Students will participate in shared reading of the rhyming book *Down by the Bay.* They will recognize rhyming words in the story. Students will listen to other pairs of words and tell if the words rhyme. Students will brainstorm a list of silly rhymes. Each student will create their own page for a class book by coming up with their own silly rhyme and writing/illlustrating it. Students will share their rhymes with the class.

Required Material:
Book *Down by the Bay* by Raffi.   Rhyming and non-rhyming picture cards.   Crayons, pencils, newsprint.

Before the Lesson:
Review the concept of rhyming words with the class. Explain that rhyming words are words that sound the same and give examples. Point out that the book we will read will have rhyming words (silly rhymes), and students should listen for words that rhyme.

During the Lesson:
Read the book *Down by the Bay* aloud to the class. Point out the first set of rhyming words and model repeating the rhyme. As we continue reading the book, invite students to read aloud together the repetitive text of the book and listen for rhymes. After the first reading, review the rhyming words from the story. Reread the book, singing the tune of *Down by the Bay.* After the second reading, show sets of picture cards to the class. Say the words aloud and ask students to put thumbs up if the words rhyme, thumbs down if they do not rhyme. Tell students that we will create our own class book of *Down by the Bay.* Brainstorm a list of silly rhymes. Students will write and illustrate their own silly rhyme for a class book.

After the Lesson:
Students will share their silly rhymes with the class. All of the student pages will be bound together in a class book. The book will be read aloud to the class during another lesson and will be placed in the library center for students to read during center time.

Assessment:
I will make observations of students during the lesson to see if they are able to recognize rhyming word pairs. I will note any important observations for student portfolios. I will assess students' individual writing and illustrations for the class book to see if they were able to make a rhyme.

Reflection:
I will review information collected from the assessment to determine if further instruction is needed for the whole group. I will determine individual students who seem to fully understand the concepts and students who need additional practice. I will plan for further instruction based on this information.

Works Consulted:
Wescott, N.B. (1987). *Raffi songs to read, Down by the bay.* Needham Heights, MA: Silver Burdett Ginn.

FIGURE 5.4. Standards-based phonological awareness lesson.

The last step, thinking ahead about how one will know whether or not the lesson was successful in helping students meet the expected level of performance, is an essential part of reflective teaching. Figure 5.4 offers an example of how one kindergarten teacher designed a standards-based lesson focused on rhyming. The reader should notice how the teacher is precise in explaining what she will do before, during, and after reading the rhyming book. In planning the lesson, she aligns the learning goal (identifying rhyming words and constructing rhymes) with the grade-level indicator, the teaching strategies she intends to use, and the assessment of student learning. Her reflection indicates that she will plan her next steps based on her observations of the students' performance, considering that some may need additional help through small-group instruction.

Field Work is relevant to everyday teaching. It is goal-driven in that it pushes for deeper thinking about literacy content and teaching and has high cognitive demand in that it requires planning, analyzing, assessing, and reflecting. The process of doing the *Field Work* provokes rich dialogue about standards, teaching, and student learning among the teachers at the next group session. As one first-grade teacher remarked:

> I have really been thinking about the focus of my instruction and just how helpful and important the standards are to my teaching. I find myself spending more time concentrating on my struggling students and how my teaching can improve their learning. I am thinking more about the practices I am using with different children. I am also learning a lot from listening to others. (*The LS Exchange*, Vol. 15, p. 7, 2003)

Examples of Making Connections

Before closing a professional development session, the literacy specialists explain not only the *Field Work* but also the *Making Connections* inquiry-based activities that are included in the materials for each session. Occasionally, teachers choose to substitute the *Making Connections* activity for the *Field Work*, especially if the activity is immediately applicable to their current situation.

Some *Making Connections* activities related to promoting schoolwide change include:

- You have been invited to make a presentation on literacy development at a districtwide parent meeting. Provide an outline of the main points of your talk.
- For the next primary-grade-level meeting, the literacy specialist has asked you to describe the importance of the alphabetic principle in learning to read. Explain to your colleagues why all teachers need to understand the alphabetic principle and show them a few strategies that

have worked well and how they can be adapted for children of all grade levels.

- You and another third-grade teacher have been invited to present to the school board some information on how teachers use standards to plan language arts instruction and assess student progress. Prepare a 5-minute presentation that convinces the board members that the standards are embedded in teachers' everyday instruction.
- Your principal has asked you to create next month's bulletin board display for the teachers' lounge. Create a chart that shows approaches to literacy education for young children and identify the benefits of each approach for children's literacy learning.
- You are the chair of the K–3 reading curriculum committee and a controversy is swirling around the extent to which oral language instruction should be represented in the curriculum. Make the case for including oral language in the curriculum at the grade level you teach based on the English language arts standards. Articulate the features of oral language teaching and learning that influence literacy achievement.

Both *Field Work* and *Making Connections* activities help professionals develop a sense of efficacy in their educator roles. Teachers' professional development is not only about observing the outcomes of effective teaching, but also about the many efforts, and the cumulative effect of them, in achieving larger school and district goals.

Extensions That Build Home–School Relationships

Building home and school connections is part of every teacher's responsibility. In their day-to-day routines, teachers plan and implement ways to connect students' in-school work with out-of-classroom practice that involves parental support and guidance. The extensions that follow the session on bridging home and school require teachers to analyze what they currently do and examine it in light of new information. By making the familiar "less familiar" and using a critical lens on what they take for granted (i.e., the usual ways of involving parents), teachers can reconstruct and reshape home learning activities into stronger and more coherent home literacy programs that further boost students' literacy learning.

Example of Field Work

During Session 8, Bridging Home and School, teachers collaborate by grade levels to plan a series of activities for parents or caregivers to use with their children at home. They first examine some essential elements of a home literacy program that promote literacy learning: explicit teaching about print, engaging children in fun and meaningful literacy practices, and providing opportunities for children to develop language skills (Lareau, 2000). Some explicit teaching activities include pointing out features of print while reading and discussing books with young children, helping them write shopping lists, and telling them what words in the environment say and mean. Parents and other caregivers engage children in fun and meaningful literacy practices when they model and explain how to question and talk about text before, during, and after reading, and when playing word games. By naming, describing, narrating, and explaining what goes on in their worlds, adults build up children's vocabulary and help them develop the concepts and language skills that support literacy development.

During the small-group problem-solving activity, the teachers brainstorm literacy activities that they have used and have found to be successful in helping children develop reading and writing skills. They select one activity that they can appropriately adapt to home environments for a parent, caregiver, or older sibling to implement. With their colleagues, they analyze the activities they selected to determine how well they meet the essential elements.

Following the session, the teachers complete the *Field Work* (Figure 5.5), which is to further develop and implement one of the activities from their group plan. As an example, Mary, a primary grade Title 1 teacher, decided to develop a series of home activities with the goal of enhancing students' comprehension of literary text, based on the work they had been doing on fairy tales. To guide her teaching and the home learning activities, she first identified the appropriate Ohio English language arts standards, benchmarks, and grade-level indicators for reading and communication.

The activities included (1) students reading a tale to parents and asking/answering questions about the characters, setting, and plot; (2) retelling a tale to a parent or sibling using a story chain they had developed in class; and (3) playing a memory game using the settings, characters, and significant events for the different tales. The culmination of the unit was a parent–child "Piggin' Out at School Night." In her *Field Work*, Mary described the activities leading up to this main event in relation to the essential elements of a home–school literacy program as shown in Figure 5.6.

As teachers share their activities at the next group session, the literacy specialists listen, take notes, and reflect on what they may need to do differently in upcoming professional development sessions to better support teachers in implementing the *Field Work*. For example, if the samples showed weak connections to the essential elements of a home–school program, the literacy specialist could provide more examples of activities to illustrate and explain the elements. They may recognize, too, that they need to provide more time to talk about spe-

Session 8—Bridging Home and School

Purpose: To design a home literacy activity that works based on evidence.

Directions: Review the essential elements necessary for planning a home literacy program. Choose an activity that would teach about print, develop language skills, and engage children in fun and meaningful literacy practices. Identify the Ohio standards, benchmarks, and grade-level indicators that are being addressed. Create the plan for parents to carry out.

Record your process below and bring your activity to share with your colleagues at the next session.

A Home Literacy Program—Essential Elements

Direct Transfer of Knowledge about Print

The Engagement of Children in Fun and Meaningful Literacy Practices

Opportunities for Children to Develop Language Skills

FIGURE 5.5. *Field Work* activity page.

Piggin' Out at School Night

Direct Transfer of Knowledge about Print:

Begin by reading a traditional version of *The Three Little Pigs* with the students in school. Have the students write a letter to their parent(s) inviting them to a "Piggin' Out at School Night." The students take the book home and read it to the parents. They also give them their invitation to the event for them to read aloud.

Engagement of Children in Fun and Meaningful Literacy Practices:

The night will begin with a dramatic reading of *The True Story of the Three Little Pigs by A. Wolf* (Scieszka, 1995). While the students read, the teachers will act it out. Then the teachers/actors will walk around while the parents and students are eating. Students will be able to ask the "wolf" and the "three little pigs" any questions they may have.

Opportunities for Children to Develop Language Skills:

When the students take a copy of the story (traditional version) home to read to their parents, they will also take home puppets for the characters. The puppets will be made in school. Students will be able to use the puppets to retell the story to their parents or any other family member or friend. Once they have attended Piggin' Out at School, they will use the puppets to retell *The True Story of the Three Little Pigs by A. Wolf* (Scieszka, 1995).

FIGURE 5.6. *Field Work* example of essential elements of home literacy program.

cific ways to evaluate the activities for what worked and what should be improved for the next home–school program or event.

Collaborative planning on *Field Work* can give teachers a jump start on the tasks that face them daily. Further, if they work as a school team, they can share the wealth of good ideas by compiling and distributing the parent–child activities to all teachers to use in workshops, conferences, open houses, and the like. Many schools and individual teachers have a parent newsletter and one or more of the activities may be featured in different issues. As literacy specialist Kay explained:

> I told my teachers they must include the three essential elements (explicit teaching, engaging in meaningful activity, and providing opportunities to develop language), and do a newsletter, but it could be done in the way *they* interpreted it . . . I told them to make it authentic, something they have done [and want to improve] or will do, not just busy work to turn in for this assignment. (*The LS Exchange*, Vol. 7, p. 4, 2001)

Other home literacy programs are more comprehensive in scope and span a year of activities and events. These are likely to involve the literacy specialist as a leader in the design, development, and implementation of these activities and events. (We provide an example of this in Chapter 6.)

Examples of Making Connections

Making Connections activities aim to stretch teachers to think more about home and school relationships and practical ways that will build those relationships.

Some examples related to home and school relationships include:

- Seeing the need to better support the parents of the English language learners in your school, you contact local agencies for literature that will acquaint them with the area and the recreational and educational opportunities. You also seek information about local interpreters and work with other teachers on a plan for sharing information with the family.
- Tape-record your discussion with a colleague about a child's progress to make yourself more aware of how you communicate such information. Self-assess your talk in relation to your word choice, tone, message, and overall affect. Reflect on what you said well and what you might need to say differently to maintain fair practice and overcome bias when communicating similar information to parents.
- The Parent Teacher Organization has invited you to speak on the importance of phonics instruction in teaching children to read. Prepare the key points of your talk and the activities that you want to explain to parents for them, in turn, to practice with their children at home.
- Plan a family literacy event. Make it a time when all families may share something about their personal traditions: recipes, albums, oral histories, written histories, scrapbooks, etc. Make sure to emphasize that these are all part of the important literacy environment of the home.

- Create activity cards for practicing literacy skills at home. At school, have each child draw one from the deck and put it in an envelope with a request for feedback from parents or caregivers when the children return the envelopes with the cards. Make the activities meaningful and connected to the children's home environment. Repeat activities that the children especially enjoy as well as ideas that put a new twist to what they do in your classroom.

Extensions That Improve Reading and Writing Instruction

Considering that learning is an individual phenomenon socially constructed through interaction with others and with the environment, we need to take into account both the social and physical elements of a setting in order to improve instruction. How the furniture is arranged, what materials are available and how they are used, and where and how students are grouped to do their work, all work to shape a learning environment. In the following extensions, we describe ways in which teachers apply what they learn in the sessions (e.g., constructing a supportive learning environment) to their own practice.

Example of Field Work

During Session 7, Preparing the Literacy Environment, the teachers study three major criteria that help guide the design of a supportive literacy learning environment: presence of print, proximity of print to children both physically and psychologically, and productivity of print for assisting children in learning to read and write (Roskos & Neuman, 2001). The literacy specialists and teachers discuss in great detail these three design criteria and how to use these criteria to assess the quality of the literacy environment (Figure 5.7).

Working in small groups, the teachers examine a set of photographs from the session materials or from local classrooms to assess the quality of the environment. They closely examine each photograph systematically for evidence of print by moving clockwise from the left-hand corner and sweeping around the space. They repeat this circular viewing process at least two or three times, making a judgment as to the quality of the design features in the environment. So that they can develop a shared understanding of the different criteria, they are required to provide a rationale for their thinking, grounded in the concrete evidence, as well as professional experience. They also interpret how learning expectations may be communicated in the particular classroom and which Ohio's English language arts standards are evidenced in the environment. From this analysis, they interpret the strengths and limitations of the environment and suggest ways that it can be improve to better support learning.

Presence of Print

There should be a widespread presence of print across settings in ways that are attractive and appealing to young children.

- At children's eye level
- Presented in a variety of formats (e.g., books, signs, children's writing, environmental print, labels, directions, etc.)
- In abundance

Proximity of Print

The literacy environment should be matched physically and psychologically to the young readers and writers using it.

- Within children's reach physically
- Safe, authentic, and useful
- Within children's grasp and rooted in real-life experiences
- Connected to children's culture, language, thinking, interests, and preferences

Productivity of Print

The literacy environment should be productive by teaching about reading and writing and communicating learning expectations.

- Lead children to new ideas about the print–sound code
- Teach children to get meaning from texts and develop habits of healthy readers and writers
- Contextualize print so children can experience print's usefulness, its pleasure, and its opportunity for personal expression

FIGURE 5.7. Design criteria for preparing the literacy environment.

Following the session, the literacy specialists explain the *Field Work*, which directs them to examine their own classrooms and take photographs of different areas. While there are multiple ways to assess literacy environments, for example, *Early Language & Literacy Classroom Observation* (ELLCO; Smith & Dickinson, 2002) and the *Classroom Literacy Environmental Profile* (CLEP; Wolfersberger, Reutzel, Sudweeks, & Fawson, 2004), this session provides a literacy environment checklist (Figure 5.8) to evaluate the quality of print evidence. Teachers are asked to assess their environment and interpret where and how the print environment communicates learning expectations (standards). After they have completed their evaluation, teachers identify special strengths and limitations and note ways to improve the quality of the literacy environment according to the design criteria.

If teachers have time before the next session, they make changes according to their plan and take another set of photographs. This time, they also observe the children and how they respond to and interact in the area that was modified. When the teachers bring their photographs and self-evaluations to the next ses-

Presence of Print	(check one)	Yes	No
Is there an abundance of print in the environment?			
Is there a variety of print? (books, signs, children's writing, environmental print, labels, directions, etc.)			
Is there print at children's eye level?			
Is the print attractive and appealing?			
Are the standards represented in the print? For example:			
Is the relative amount of commercial print greater than 75%?			
Is the relative amount of teacher-made print greater than 75%?			
Is the relative amount of child-made print greater than 75%?			
Strengths and Limitations:			
Suggested Improvements:			

Proximity of Print	(check one)	Yes	No
Is print useful, safe, and authentic?			
Is the print within the children's reach physically?			
Is the print within the children's grasp and rooted in real-life experiences?			
Is the print connected to children's culture, language, thinking, and interests?			
Is the display of standards within the children's grasp? For example:			
Strengths and Limitations:			
Suggested Improvements:			

Productivity of Print	(check one)	Yes	No
Does the print lead children to new ideas about the print–sound code?			
Does the print teach children to get meaning from texts and develop habits of healthy readers and writers?			
Does the print encourage children to develop habits of healthy readers and writers?			
Is the print in a context that allows children to experience its usefulness, pleasure, and opportunity for expression?			
Does the print show evidence of the children meeting learning expectations? For example:			
Strengths and Limitations:			
Suggested Improvements:			

FIGURE 5.8. Literacy environment checklist.

sion, they are excited to share their discoveries and discuss precisely what changes they made or will make to improve the environment.

Examples of Making Connections

Making Connections activities extend learning about reading and writing instruction and also provide opportunities for teachers to make public some of the products of their learning. These kinds of activities foster a learning community of teachers and students in a school.

Some examples that extend learning about reading and writing include:

- Create a photo essay to display outside your classroom door that highlights your classroom as a literacy rich environment. Invite the children to participate in taking photos, selecting photographs, and developing text for the essay.
- Examine your classroom environment for evidence of student writing and ways that you draw their attention to it. Make a change that you think will elicit positive observations or inquiry from students. Observe what students say and do and share your observations with another teacher.
- Assess how much the book corner or reading area of your classroom is utilized by the students. Talk with a colleague about ways to make it more inviting and productive. Make a specific plan with the students and implement one change at a time. Devise a way to keep track of how much it is used to involve the students in the monitoring process.
- Design posters or other displays for your classroom that illustrate some of the strategies you learn about in the sessions. For example, show the strategic questions that provoke critical thinking about text in a Directed Reading–Thinking Activity (DRTA; Stauffer, 1975): *What do you think will happen? Why do you think so? How can you prove it?*
- Questioning is a common teaching strategy. Its effectiveness depends on the types of questions asked and how often, as well as by whom—teachers and/or children. To gauge how well your questioning works in helping children to talk on their own and elaborate their responses, design a discourse map for your small-group work. Create a simple diagram of the table and the seating arrangement and a simple coding scheme for who talks, type of question, and response. Keep track of the dialogue yourself during the lesson or ask a colleague to keep track for you. Analyze the record and make changes that will encourage more elaborated and critical responses from students. Use the discourse map a few more times to observe how the changes affect student performance.

CLOSING

In this chapter, we discussed the importance of the connection between concepts examined in the professional development setting and everyday teaching work. We illustrated many examples of extension activities in the professional development model of the LS Project, which we organized as extensions for supporting schoolwide change, home–school relationships, and the learning environment. These activities dovetail with and extend the problem-solving activity of a professional development session, assuring a tight connection between learning in the session and deepening learning through practice. Void of this critical component, professional development activity will not sustain or deepen learning. Through meaningful applications of what teachers study and do in a group setting to their own instructional settings, teachers develop an enthusiasm for professional learning, realize the fruits of their labor, and strengthen the educational community.

In Chapter 6, we illuminate other extensions of the professional development sessions, focusing specifically on the coaching role that literacy specialists can and do play as they assist teachers in implementing the extension activities. We will observe from a broad perspective how a literacy specialist takes a leading role in collaborating with teachers on a schoolwide literacy event. We will then narrow our lens on coaching as we describe how a literacy specialist and teacher coplan a standards-based lesson, one of the *Field Work* activities. Getting deeper into practice, we take our readers inside classroom instruction and the surrounding coaching conversations in a *Field Work* activity that follows Session 11, Teaching Comprehension, to observe a literacy specialist working alongside a teacher to improve her reading instruction.

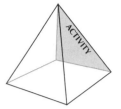

CHAPTER 6

Coaching to Improve Practice

Holding Meetings Around a Shared Goal	Coplanning Lessons	Analyzing Teaching	Considerations in Using Inquiry Tools

The end result is to reach our destination and the goal of empowerment of student learning by keeping an "eye on children learning," keeping that at the center, and helping them achieve at the highest potential levels. This can be accomplished by providing teachers with the tools to create an environment of opportunities to learn. The tools are based on research and what we know about how children learn, which is not a one size fits all.

—*The LS Exchange* (Vol. 18, p. 2, 2004)

In this chapter, we continue to illustrate how the foundational tenets guide the professional development of the LS Project. As stated in Chapter 1, these tenets assume a new role for literacy specialists as teachers of teachers. Literacy specialists in the LS Project take on Levels 1, 2, or 3 of coaching activities as described in *The Role and Qualifications of the Reading Coach in the United States: A Position Statement of the International Reading Association* (International Reading Association, 2004b). They engage in many informal activities (Level 1), such as providing resources, making presentations, and assisting teachers with various aspects of assessment, planning, and instruction. More formally (Level

2), literacy specialists coach teachers through small group activities that take place during the professional development sessions and extension activities. Many literacy specialists have the opportunity to engage with teachers in more intense, one-on-one conversations and activities focused on analysis of teaching (Level 3).

The professional development sessions centered on the core curriculum provide a structure for assisting teachers in gaining new knowledge about literacy content and in making shifts in practice that will advance student learning. Coaching that focuses specifically on instructional improvements occur primarily through the *Field Work* experiences. In the following examples, we illustrate some of the ways that the literacy specialists coach through *Field Work*.

HOLDING MEETINGS AROUND A SHARED GOAL

In the following example of literacy coaching through *Field Work*, we show how the literacy specialist is one member of a teacher group who work as a team to develop a cohesive home literacy program that includes the essential elements of family literacy and building communities. This activity may be considered a Level 2 coaching activity, that is, holding a team meeting for the purpose of achieving a shared goal.

Marian, a literacy specialist, works with a team of kindergarten teachers and the Title I teacher to develop a program designed to assist parents in making their children's first year of school a positive experience for both the children and the parents. The program consists of four in-school sessions that include parenting tips, learning and teaching strategies, question and answer periods, and sharing time with children. Presentations focus on reading, math, and writing. The sessions also involve other staff members, volunteers, kindergartners, and older students.

In the following vignette, we observe a session focused on how to support children's writing development. We see that the teachers, literacy specialist, children, and parents all have an active role in the session.

Parents Learn about Writing Development

The kindergarten parents gather for their third meeting of the year, which focuses on writing. Marian begins with a discussion of writing development and its connection to reading. She distributes a writing booklet that shows writing samples for different phases of development. She encourages parents to examine their children's writing (Figure 6.1), praise them for their attempts and encourage them to continue writing. She explains that this will help the children associate writing with positive parental attention.

"I went to a cookout"

"I like to ride my bike"

"Horse"

FIGURE 6.1. Children's writing samples.

Parents Learn That Explicit Teaching is Important

Next, Lora, a kindergarten teacher, reads to the children and parents *Click, Clack, Moo* (Cronin, 2000), a story that shows that reading and writing are directly connected. Lora stresses with parents the importance of reading books to their children at home and points out how speaking, reading, and writing are part of daily life.

Parents Experience Fun and Meaningful Practices

Lora then gives the parents their own copy of the book along with a writing bag that includes paper, pencils, erasers, sharpeners, letter formation paper, and a calendar of writing prompts to use each week of the month. As the parents sit alongside their children on the carpet, Lora tells them that they will find out more about what to do with these items after they listen to their children read some of their journal entries.

Parents Observe the Reciprocal Relationship in Writing and Language Development

Next, the parents and some of the children are asked to move to the tables facing the front of the room and watch as another teacher, Roberta, demonstrates a writing lesson with five children. Roberta shows the children a big picture of many farm animals and asks individual children to tell one thing about one of the animals. After each has a turn, she tells them to say aloud what they are going to write. One-by-one, she orally repeats the children's sentences, allowing them to hear what their thoughts sound like and making it easier for them to remember what they are going to write. After they have all started writing, Roberta says quietly to the parents and the other children that the students are developing language skills as they take their ideas and form complete sentences before writing them. The children then take turns reading their sentences to each other. She points out that this is a technique they can use at home when involving children in writing letters, grocery lists, reminder notes, and the like. At the close of the session, there is a question and answer period.

Before leaving, the parents complete an evaluation of the session, indicating what they found useful, what more they would like to know, and what they plan to do for follow through with their children. The team then uses that information to plan the specifics of their next session. (Adapted from Session 8 *Field Work* submitted by Lora, Title I teacher.)

Notice that in this situation, the literacy specialist has an opportunity to further develop her teaching skills when she takes what she has explained to teachers in the professional development session and adapts it for a parent audience. The teachers have an opportunity to not only see how Marian explains literacy concepts to parents, but they also have her support as they, too, demonstrate and explain instructional strategies.

As this example shows, the literacy specialist's activities around home–school connections are collaborative among many teachers, other specialists, and school administrators. Viewed as highly knowledgeable professionals in literacy by their colleagues, literacy specialists serve as valuable resource experts who can lead schoolwide literacy efforts. In their daily interactions with teachers, they may participate in parent conferences and coach teachers in making goal oriented, explicit, meaningful, and engaging literacy connections to the home environment.

COPLANNING LESSONS

In Chapter 5, we discussed an example of a *Field Work* extension that requires teachers to plan and implement a standards-based lesson. We showed how the *Field Work* creates an authentic literacy coaching context for the literacy specialist to collaborate with one or more teachers. For the teachers, what to do is made clear by the procedures and the accompanying worksheets that guide the implementation. Less clear is what the literacy specialist can do to assist the teacher.

The next example of a Level 2 literacy coaching activity is more formal than the group meeting. This one involves coplanning a standards-based lesson. The first step is for the literacy specialists to ask for one or more teachers to work together on the *Field Work* and establish a meeting time to discuss the activity. At the initial meeting, the teacher and literacy specialist work through the lesson plan template (Figure 6.2) to design the lesson.

At first glance, the process of completing the template seems relatively straightforward. After the plan is technically completed, the literacy specialist engages the teacher in analyzing the plan. Through a series of well-crafted questions, the literacy specialist raises the cognitive power of the task from procedural to analytical to reflective. The following questions help guide the analysis:

- How does the lesson goal align with the learning expectations?
- Are the materials on the students' instructional level? How do you know?
- How will the teaching strategies develop the particular literacy concept or skill?
- What are the methods for assessing student learning?
- How will data be collected systematically during instruction as well as after the lesson?
- What are the methods for self-critiquing your teaching?
- How will you know what to retain and what to change in the next lesson?

Within the next week after the planning meeting, the teacher teaches the lesson and collects samples of student work to assess student performance. The teacher reflects on how well the students performed and how well the lesson was implemented according to its design. Following the lesson, the literacy specialist and teacher meet to discuss the lesson. The following questions help guide this discussion:

- Was the goal of the lesson achieved? How do you know?
- What teaching strategies did you use?
- Do you think the strategies were effective? How do you know?
- What might you do differently in the next lesson?
- How do you think the change will affect student performance?
- What are your next steps?

The planning and debriefing conversations that center on these questions are quite detailed and substantive. They cannot happen on the run. Instead, they require the literacy specialist to strategize about how to begin the conversation, how to frame the questions, and how to respond to teachers' comments, debates,

TEACHING ENGLISH LANGUAGE ARTS
LESSON PLAN TEMPLATE

English Language Arts Standard:

Benchmark:

Grade-Level Indicator(s):

Focus of Instruction:

Description of Lesson:

Required Material:

Before the Lesson:

During the Lesson:

After the Lesson:

Assessment:

Reflection:

Works Consulted:

FIGURE 6.2. Lesson plan template.

inquiries, and suggestions. At the end of the postlesson conference, the literacy specialist asks the teacher to share his or her lesson reflections and the coaching experience with other teachers to jump-start the next professional development session. If all of the teachers in the professional development session were to take turns or jointly inquire into their own practice to this extent, then surely the professional learning community would be enriched (and energized).

ANALYZING TEACHING

Although teachers may choose to implement any of the *Field Work* suggestions individually, with another teacher, or with a literacy specialist, the *Field Work* in the teaching domain lends itself to one-on-one collaboration between a literacy specialist and a teacher. In this next example, we observe an even more intense and formal Level 3 coaching activity. A literacy specialist, Linda, collaborates with a teacher, Sharon, to closely examine a lesson on retelling that she implemented with a small group of first-grade students.

To set the stage, we need to start from the *During* segment of professional development Session 11, Teaching Reading Comprehension. During this session, teachers work as partners to analyze a comprehension lesson. They begin by examining the lesson plan and viewing a video segment of a second-grade standards-based reading lesson on using context clues to infer the meaning of unfamiliar vocabulary. The purpose of this problem-solving activity is to understand that effective teaching involves both skillful use of protocols and scaffolds that assist students' performance. Recall from Chapter 2 that a *protocol* is a blueprint for action, such as the steps for a Directed Reading–Thinking Activity (DRTA; Stauffer, 1975) or the steps in a words-in-context strategy. Teacher talk and teacher–student interaction make visible the protocol in the back-and-forth of asking, answering, explaining, clarifying, interpreting, and so forth. The scaffolding features that support students' understanding of a task are evidenced in how the teacher involves students in the task and assists them in achieving the learning goal (Figure 6.3).

Before watching the video, teachers read the sample analytical guide to get an idea of the lesson and to predict what they would expect to see in the video. The protocol and scaffolding features for a teaching words-in-context strategy are illustrated in Figure 6.4.

The teachers then view a 5-minute segment and take notes as they observe. After viewing, they share their observations and respond to the following questions:

- What were the students saying and doing?
- What were the specific teaching actions in the protocol that you observed?
- What evidence of scaffolding did you observe?

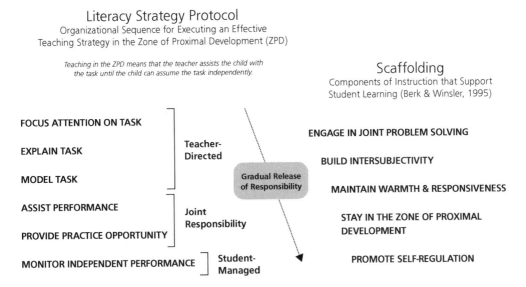

FIGURE 6.3. Protocol and scaffolding features evident in effective teaching strategies.

The literacy specialist shows the video again, but this time provides a transcript of the lesson so that teachers can observe the instruction more closely. The literacy specialist tells the teachers to watch for the teacher's execution of the words-in-context protocol, the scaffolds that assist the students in using the strategy to figure out unfamiliar words, and evidence of students' efforts at grasping the strategy.

Next, teachers engage in a fine-grained analysis of the teaching by coding the transcript. They refer to the guide for analyzing a words-in-context lesson for the coding scheme. Evidence of protocol features they mark as P1, P2, P3, and so on, and evidence of scaffolding as S1, S2, S3, and so on, depending on the specific actions and interactions they observe. After this close analysis, the partners compare their observations and discuss how well the strategy was implemented. This process of closely examining a lesson and learning what to look for pushes teachers to achieve a deeper understanding of teaching reading and writing.

In the *Field Work* that follows the session, the teachers plan and implement a standards-based vocabulary or text comprehension lesson using one of the strategies studied in the session: semantic mapping (e.g., word web), predict/confirm/integrate strategy (e.g., DRTA, K–W–L), retelling strategy (e.g., story mapping), or words-in-context strategy (e.g., cloze).

The general procedures for carrying out this *Field Work* include:

1. Plan the standards-based lesson.
2. Teach the lesson and audiotape it. (Teachers are also encouraged to videotape a lesson for analysis, although this step requires more preparation and is not as feasible as audiotaping.)

Focus of Reading Instruction: Comprehension

Specific Strategy: Using context clues to figure out the meaning of unknown words during reading

Protocol (P) Features:

PI Interest children in a book.

P2 Model using context clues to figure out the meaning of an unknown word.

P3 Engage children in reading the book.

P4 Provide opportunities for practice in using context clues.

P5 Monitor independent performance and give feedback.

Scaffolding (S) Features:

SI Joint problem solving (involving children in meaningful activity; helping children learn by doing)

S2 Intersubjectivity (coming to a shared understanding; working toward a shared goal)

S3 Warmth and responsiveness (creating a positive emotional tone; providing verbal praise; attributing competence to children)

S4 Staying in the ZPD (organizing activities that are challenging for children, but achievable by them with assistance; using instructional talk that prompts them to talk, encourages them to tell more, and adds to their thoughts and ideas)

S5 Self-regulation (stepping back to let children take control of their own activity; providing assistance as needed to support children's problem solving)

(See Berk & Winsler, 1995)

FIGURE 6.4. Guide for analyzing words in context lesson.

3. Listen to the recording and select 5–10 minutes that represent ample teacher–student interaction.
4. Prepare a written transcript of the teaching segment.
5. Mark the transcript using the protocol and scaffolding codes.
6. Record statements that summarize their own observations of their own teaching.
7. Write a brief reflection that discusses their own interpretations of the lesson.
8. Bring the coded transcript, the lesson plan, their reflection, and any artifacts of the lesson to the next session.

These procedures, when carried out collaboratively by the literacy specialist and the teacher, set up the conditions for a dialogue wherein one professional assists another in closely analyzing teaching. The literacy specialist and the teacher talk specifically about reading and writing instruction in relation to how well the students perform and the specific teaching actions that support the students' understanding of the concept or strategy. The cognitive task central to the conversation is a close analysis of a lesson transcript to determine what works in a lesson, what does not work, and how to identify what changes are needed to improve the lesson. The transcript provides a tangible record of the teaching, the "something specific to talk about," and thereby distances the teaching from the teacher. This "distancing" allows for a more objective analysis of a lesson so that the literacy specialist and the teacher can achieve a keener understanding of the lesson and a clearer recognition of specifically what to do next to better support students' learning. This process of collaborative inquiry, briefly described here, is organized around the Teacher Learning Instrument (TLI), which has been developed as a research-based tool for improving teaching (Rosemary, 2005).

When the literacy specialist coaches a teacher on improving a lesson using the *Field Work* activities in the teaching domain, together they follow these steps:

- *Step 1: Plan Together.* The teacher and the literacy specialist plan a literacy lesson using a planning guide like the one illustrated in the previous section. They begin by identifying the instructional focus (e.g., comprehension) and a teaching strategy for improvement (e.g., DRTA, story map, retelling). They discuss the strategy in terms of when to use it, with whom, and why, and then outline the teaching actions or the protocol for implementing it. They also discuss how the teacher plans to support students' learning by discussing the scaffolding features.

- *Step 2: Teacher Teaches.* In preparation for audiotaping the lesson, the teacher places a microrecorder in his or her pocket and clips a lavaliere microphone to his or her clothing close to his or her face to assure clear audio. The teacher then teaches the lesson.

- *Step 3: Analyze Independently.* As soon as possible following the lesson, the teacher listens to the lesson and transcribes a 10-minute segment containing ample teacher–student interactions. This process of transcribing, although relatively tedious and time-consuming, calls for close listening, pausing, writing, and so forth. This iterative process serves as a powerful mediator for reflecting, looking back, and structuring the teacher's thinking about his or her teaching. The literacy specialist can assist with the process by teaching the students while the teacher transcribes. Sometimes the literacy specialist may transcribe the tape or part of the tape for the teacher, or they may do the transcribing together.

Next, the literacy specialist and the teacher independently analyze their copies of the transcript. Having practiced coding a transcript during the professional development session, the literacy specialist and the teacher independently code their own copy of the transcript before coming together to discuss the lesson.

After coding, the teacher writes statements summarizing his or her analysis. These may relate to how often some codes are used (e.g., "The scaffolding feature I used the most was warmth and responsiveness"); patterns observed in the teacher's talk (e.g., "My questions were mostly yes- or no-type questions and required very short responses from the students"), and the student's talk (e.g., "The student started the session with some elaborated responses but reverted back to short answers toward the end of the session"). Other elements of the instruction may also be discussed, such as the degree of text difficulty, grouping arrangement, student materials or props, and particular parts of the lesson (e.g., "At the beginning of the lesson, I reminded the students of the previous lesson and our continuous focus on fluency").

• *Step 4: Reflect Independently.* In addition to writing a summary of the analysis, the teacher and the literacy specialist each write their own reflections on the lesson. The written summary and the reflection are important parts of the TLI process. Whereas coding is a microanalysis to identify protocol and scaffolding features in the actual teaching compared to the intended teaching actions listed in the planning guide, the written summary and the reflection reveal the teacher's thinking about what he or she understands about his or her teaching—a macrolevel synthesis of what is understood about teaching. For the coach, writing a reflection helps him or her to think through the lesson from the lesson-planning phase to the teaching, and then to planning what to say in the upcoming debriefing conversation with the teacher.

• *Step 5: Debrief Together.* Within a week of the lesson, the teacher and the literacy specialist meet to discuss the lesson. They bring their coded transcripts along with any relevant artifacts of the lesson to their meeting. These conversations take the independent analyses to a level of collaborative problem solving. It is in the postlesson conversation that metacognitive processes are exposed: They think aloud about their thinking, which creates a search for deeper understanding about how to improve teaching and learning.

Now, let's follow the TLI process in action through the lenses of a literacy specialist, Linda, and a Title I teacher, Sharon, as they debrief after Sharon's retelling lesson that she implemented with a small group of first-grade students. (The data used in this example are taken from a study of TLI in Rosemary, Freppon, & Kinnucan-Welsch, 2002.) The analytical guide for that lesson is presented in Figure 6.5. Linda, the literacy specialist, provides a synopsis of the lesson and the learning expectations:

Sharon chose to have her small group of Title I first graders participate in the retelling of the story *The Elves and the Shoemaker.* Before engaging them in the retelling, she read the story to them. In addition to reading them the story, she encouraged them to compare this story to one read the day before and

Area of Reading Instruction: Comprehension

Specific Strategy: Retelling Using Puppets

Protocol (P) Features:

PI Use a prop to retell a familiar story.

P2 Model narrative language in the retelling.

P3 Engage students in the retelling.

P4 Provide opportunities for practicing and retelling.

P5 Monitor independent performance and give feedback.

Scaffolding (S) Features:

SI Joint problem solving (involving children in meaningful activity; helping children learn by doing)

S2 Intersubjectivity (coming to a shared understanding; working toward a shared goal)

S3 Warmth and responsiveness (creating a positive emotional tone; providing verbal praise; attributing competence to children)

S4 Staying in the ZPD (organizing activities that are challenging for children, but achievable by them with assistance; using instructional talk that prompts them to talk, encourages them to tell more, and adds to their thoughts and ideas)

S5 Self-regulation (stepping back to let children take control of their own activity; providing assistance as needed to support children's problem solving)

(See Berk & Winsler, 1995)

FIGURE 6.5. Guide for analyzing retelling a familiar narrative lesson.

used a character web to compare and contrast characteristics of "good elves" and "bad elves." She reminded them to pay attention to how she read and how she used her voice to create characters.

During the reading of the story to them, she called their attention to the facts about elves that they had listed the previous day. She made a link between prior knowledge and the new story—that is, a text-to-text and a text-to-self connection. She attempted a simplified oral version of the cloze procedure when reading the text, allowing the students time to complete the missing words. This procedure was designed to have the students supply the words and phrases, such as "Once upon a time" and so on associated with storytelling.

After reading, she distributed stick puppets to aid them in the retelling. The students retold the story while using a puppet, each student having his or her own puppet character. The teacher expected that the students would project other people's feelings through the use of narrative language and storytelling. She also expected proper sequencing.

Starting with Talking about Impressions of the Lesson

The next day, after Sharon taught the lesson, she and Linda met to discuss their observations and interpretations. Their conversation began with sharing their general impressions of how the lesson went.

LINDA: I think the first thing I would like to talk about is your overall impression of how we think this went and take a look at, thinking back, at how you originally envisioned this lesson was going and then some of the things that happened as planned and then some of the things that happened as things do when you work with kids.

SHARON: Okay, I had hoped that because I was using what I thought was a familiar story, *The Elves and the Shoemaker* [Galdone, 1986], and because I was giving them puppets to work with, stick puppets, and because I didn't think they had a lot of opportunity to do something like that, I thought they would be more engaged, more anxious to retell the story, when in fact, I don't think I ever actually got to a P5. [See Figure 6.5; the Protocol feature P5 is "monitor independent performance and give feedback."]

LINDA: But I noticed in your approach, and I think the children's frustration came out later when they started to, you know, beat each other up with their little stick puppets. They probably, at this point, were not catching on—at least, that's my impression. So, when I looked through and coded these things, I found, actually, evidence of all of the protocol descriptors, the P1 through P5 and I found all of the scaffolding. But I did not notice in your attempt to engage them, which is a lot of them, because they were not very engaged, that you spent a lot of time trying to get them, what were those, the S4, you know the ZPD, because you were very frequently giving them starts to sentences, helping them along, giving them the opportunity to get engaged. There was a lot of that going on. I think that's what we do when we start to become very aware of what needs to happen in order to make a change in our lesson, and still that wasn't working. So, let's talk a little bit about that because there were things that did work, but there were other things that probably could be adapted a little better.

SHARON: I wanted to give them encouragement and I wanted to applaud them for their efforts, but I never even had the opportunity to do that. You're right. It was just turning into frustration and so I tried to pick something that was challenging. Maybe I should have picked a much more familiar story so they could have carried the story without my support as much as I did.

LINDA: I kind of got the sense that they didn't know exactly how to go about retelling a story with puppets. Since I wasn't there, I got the sense that they were doing things with the puppets. They were thinking and therefore engaged at the thinking level of the story, but not at the level you wanted them to where they were actually going to talk, which is the purpose of the lesson—to engage them in the dialogue.

Let's pause here and analyze what has happened so far. Linda opens the conversation by gently prompting Sharon to give her overall impressions of how the lesson went. Sharon had many different thoughts: about her story selection, about using the puppets, about the children not being engaged, and about how she could not get them to retell some of the story on their own and give them feedback. Linda then shifted the conversation to evidence of what she thought went well and how Sharon had executed the protocol according to her plan. She even mentioned that she had attempted to give the students lots of prompts to help them in the retelling, which she noted was working in the students' ZPD. Linda pointed out that giving lots of assistance is what teachers do when they realize that the task they have given to the students is too difficult. She suggests that they stay with this point and talk more about what was working and what could be improved. Notice that the focus of this conversation is on the students' performance and the teacher's moves that more or less supported their ability to meet the learning expectation, which was *use the dialogue* of a story in their retelling.

Analyzing: Thinking about Teaching

In the next part, we see that Linda and Sharon zero in on their coding of the lesson transcript. This takes them to a deeper level of analysis where they share their findings (codes) and explain their thinking.

LINDA: Let's turn our attention to the actual teacher and student responses. Let's see if we can come to agreement on what we found.

SHARON: I found myself giving myself a lot of P1's, where I am trying to focus the attention on using oral language, or P3's, on what I was trying to model, and I found myself again carrying the lesson, trying to "pull" the activity out of them. They never took any ownership of it.

LINDA: Right. I found, interestingly enough, and maybe it was just a matter of interpretation, I found more P3's, which is . . .

SHARON: Modeling the talk.

LINDA: Yes, because you were giving them a lot of starter sentences and asking them to come up with a missing word, and they even found that difficult. I know we had a few laughs during this because it was very comical, some of the responses that you did get. If you look at the whole lesson, I think that your attempts to model the language was very appropriate, but they were not responding. How about scaffolding?

SHARON: Staying in the ZPD—it had to be challenging to encourage them to tell more but it just wasn't working. Maybe I just wasn't in the zone.

LINDA: I saw at least four or five examples of your trying to get them to tell more, but I agree that they are not in their ZPD. I think you were trying to make it achievable for them, assisting them and giving them prompts to talk more. There is a lot of that going on in your attempts to have them understand what you wanted them to do.

As their conversation focused on a closer analysis of the teacher–student interaction, they arrived at a shared understanding of what had occurred in the lesson. In the next part of the transcript, we observe how Linda assisted Sharon in thinking through what she should do next time to better support students' learning.

LINDA: What I would like to get to before we finish today is how we can make plans to address the issue of ZPD with these children. I think that that was probably, in my experience, that if things don't go well, it's probably that they do not know what to expect to do or it was too much. What story do you think you might do?

SHARON: *The Little Red Hen.* As I read it to them, I will engage them in the responses of *The Little Red Hen*, and so when they say, "Not I, said the cat, not I said the dog," we will already be rehearsing it before we do that in the retelling.

LINDA: So you're going to use a more predictable book. I think that will probably be a good start with them. The other thing I am wondering about is, perhaps you might want to consider reading the story the session before. What do you think about actually modeling the retelling with the stick puppets so they could actually see what a retelling looks like?

SHARON: Oh, all right, that sounds like an excellent idea.

LINDA: The one lesson would be to go through *The Little Red Hen* and go through [modeling] while you're reading it to them.

SHARON: Yes, and familiarize them with it.

LINDA: And then, maybe in the next lesson, get them to do the retelling you wanted them to do in this lesson. You might have some time, because you see them almost every day, to kind of give them more practice. That's what they seemed to need, more practice with the retelling. What I'm trying to say is let's see if by putting in more time for them to see you model this, and let's see what they do. I think that your goal was to get them all to participate.

SHARON: Exactly.

In this part of the postlesson conversation, the literacy specialist and the teacher get to the details of how to work within the students' ZPD. Through Linda's open-ended questioning, clarifying, and providing feedback, she assists Sharon in figuring out how she can teach a retelling lesson next time so that the students will be more successful. Sharon explained how she will need to choose a more familiar text, model the use of puppets, and provide more practice—all of which indicate intentional shifts on her part to lead the students to independent performance of the task.

What has been discussed so far is how the TLI process engages a literacy specialist and a teacher in thinking about teaching, which is a metacognitive process. On a procedural level, their conversations illustrate their thinking about how to accomplish the cognitive goal of comparing their coding of a lesson transcript. After this task is accomplished, the literacy specialist and the teacher delve into talking about what their analyses mean. In doing so, they deepen understanding of the lesson.

Reflecting: Thinking about Learning in Teaching

The coded lesson transcripts, as tangible records of the teaching, serve as the object of inquiry, distancing the teacher from the teaching. This analysis slows down the teaching process so that the teacher can become more aware of the students' actions and interactions. She can observe in the tangible record what she could not have observed during the actual teaching of the lesson. She, with her coach, can go back and forth from the plan, to the learning goal, to her own and students' actions and their interactions.

In getting the most benefit from the TLI process, the literacy specialist and the teacher engage in the process a few more times. They maintain the same instructional focus and teaching strategy that they selected from the outset of the process. In each subsequent debriefing conversation (as with the first one), the literacy specialist asks the teacher to review the learning goal, the strategy, and the rationale for using the particular strategy for the particular group of students. The aim is to keep the focus on the students' performance as a window into how to hone the teaching.

In this next excerpt taken from the second debriefing conversation between Linda and Sharon, Linda begins the conversation, as she did after the first lesson, by asking Sharon to give her impressions of the second lesson on retelling. The teacher verbalizes her thinking about her own and her students' actions. She uses details of the second lesson transcript to illuminate her new thoughts about what had occurred and how she could change her instruction further to help the students reach the goal of independently producing an accurate and affective retelling of a familiar story.

LINDA: Would you please refresh my memory about some of the things we had talked about in the first lesson and how you were going to make the changes with this next lesson?

SHARON: All right, first of all the material was too difficult for my students. It was a story that, although I was familiar with it, the students were not. The dialogue did not happen even with repetition of it, so it was difficult for them to catch on to the phrasing. I drove the majority of the entire play by jumping in and trying to get them the language, feed them the directions, and so forth, primarily driven by myself. So spending time doing the [retelling] protocol, I chose *The Three Little Pigs* this time to give them a more familiar story. [Notice that Sharon did not follow through with the *Little Red Hen*. She found that this, too, was too difficult for the students.] I still found myself jumping in and providing dialogue, providing transitional phrases, hoping they would do more on their own. But they still were not quite there.

LINDA: Talk a little bit about the modeling that might have occurred in this one as compared to the first lesson. I think we both talked about that there was a need for you to do more modeling of that language.

SHARON: Right, I did. I read the story to them as I was telling them the story. I acted it out with the puppets so they could see what their puppets might be doing while they were speaking.

LINDA: As I look at the transcript [of the second lesson], I do see more of the modeling of the language so they were hearing from you and then knowing what you were going to expect and how they were going to participate. What do you think of the ZPD issue, because that was such a big one from the last time?

SHARON: It's very important that they have to understand the language, understand the story elements, the problem and the solution, and, at the same time, have a clear sense of what they are going to be doing.

LINDA: So, the feeling is that this story was much more at their level and because of that they had more opportunity to participate.

SHARON: And confidence.

By the end of the second debriefing conversation, Sharon realized that she still needed to let them take ownership: "It was a gradual process but I looked at that and thought, I am not there yet, but a little closer to it." Sharon's next steps were to identify a shorter, simpler narrative, and to continue modeling and providing lots of practice until her students could successfully enact the retelling using both story language and voice.

After all of the adjustments that Sharon made to better teach within the students' ZPD, she and Linda deemed the third lesson a success. Linda asked

Sharon to explain what made the third lesson more successful than the other two, and Sharon responded:

> The text was much more appropriate, the dialogue was repetitive and easier for them to remember. And again, I modeled the story using the puppets. I read it first, and then I gave it to them to rehearse so they had a lot more repetition.

Ultimately, in using the TLI, the literacy specialist and the teacher have a shared goal of making adjustments in teaching that will result in improved student performance. As we saw in the case of Linda and Sharon, their conversations that surrounded the analysis of the transcript focused on this goal and led to a deeper understanding of the interplay between teaching and learning.

CONSIDERATIONS IN USING INQUIRY TOOLS

In the TLI case we presented here, we see that the process of lesson analysis is a collaborative inquiry between colleagues. Even though Sharon and Linda appeared to be well versed in reading content and pedagogy, they found themselves learning even more about effective teaching strategies. This example shows that teachers who are willing to engage in self-examination of their own teaching with a knowledgeable and skillful coach can use what they learn to self-regulate their teaching and to make significant shifts in their practice that will boost student learning.

We have some research to suggest that the TLI is a viable inquiry tool for assisting teachers in developing a self-monitoring stance toward their own teaching (Rosemary, 2005; Rosemary et al., 2002). We explain that research in Chapter 8. Here we provide a list of research-based considerations for use of the TLI in multiple instructional contexts.

- The TLI process can better serve as a tool for teaching improvement when the literacy coach has a solid grounding in research-based reading strategies and a firm grasp of the concept of scaffolding.
- The process of transcript coding is in itself a cognitive activity that may need to be scaffolded at the outset of the process. The coach–teacher conversations rely heavily on the coded transcript, and thus the quality of the conversation that surrounds the transcript depends on an accurate transcript and keen observers.
- The additional time and effort required for transcribing needs to be considered. Transcribing even 10-minute excerpts from lessons is additional work for the teacher. In university clinical settings, this work is typically an assignment. Ways to support classroom teachers in this process need to be considered.

For example, a coach may help the teacher find the time to transcribe by teaching the students while the teacher transcribes or transcribing for the teacher, although this limits the teacher's opportunity to review the lesson firsthand. An administrator, who sees this as a valuable part of professional development, can also support the process by scheduling time for teachers to do this transcribing during their work day.

• Fundamentally, the teacher–coach relationship must be built on mutual trust and valued by all involved.

Inquiry processes, such as the TLI, that zero in on students' understanding and misunderstanding can help teachers see themselves as mediators of student learning. Outside of literacy teaching, in mathematics (Crockett, 2002; Fernandez, Cannon, & Chokshi, 2003; Hiebert & Stigler, 2000) and in science education (Sandoval, Deneroff, & Franke, 2002), for example, there is evidence that teachers' examination of student work creates a "problem" to be solved that can lead to better lesson planning and implementation. These kinds of inquiry tools help teachers to see for themselves how their instructional decisions impact student learning. Further, to maximize the benefits of inquiry tools, teachers fundamentally need to know how to systematically gather and interpret information about students' needs. They need to know (1) how to use a variety of appropriate assessments, (2) how to analyze and interpret data, and (3) how to plan and implement effective reading and writing instruction. Thus, inquiry processes can further scaffold teachers toward more skilled teaching when professional development also takes into account the development of teachers' knowledge of their students, subject matter, and pedagogy.

CLOSING

In this chapter, we described how extension activities expand professional learning opportunities for all involved by setting up a coaching context for further collaborative inquiry. A teacher and a literacy specialist or other colleague work side by side with the ultimate goal of improving instruction in ways that bolster student achievement. Our examples illuminated the kinds of coaching activities that literacy specialists engage in with teachers. In the LS Project, they lead and assist teachers in achieving broader schoolwide goals and also more individualized goals centered on improving teaching.

In the next chapter, we shift our focus from the learning network and activity to a focus on accountability and other practical matters. We discuss the nuts-and-bolts of launching and sustaining the LS Project, a comprehensive, large-scale model of professional development.

CHAPTER 7

Accountability and Other Practical Matters

Accountability in Professional Development	Accountability in the Litearcy Specialist Project	Other Practical Matters

> When I arrived at Hill View Elementary, a first-grade teacher greeted me at the door letting me know that she would like to be part of the Literacy Specialist Project. After checking my voicemail messages, I was happy to hear a message from a third-grade team of five teachers wanting to be involved as well! I had quickly raised my number of participants from five to fifteen.
>
> —*The LS Exchange* (Vol. 17, p. 5, 2004)

In our account of the LS Project thus far, we have described the goal and the underlying tenets of this professional development initiative, both of which center on a core curriculum for K–3 educators. We have explained the content, the design, and the network structure for disseminating the curriculum across the learning networks of field faculty, literacy specialists, and teachers. We brought you face to face with these key players so that you could observe their activity inside the learning contexts of field faculty meetings, literacy specialist sessions with teachers, and classrooms, where the participating teachers apply what they learn to their own practice with the goal of honing their instruction to bolster student performance. Our account would be incomplete, however, without a discussion of accountability and other practical matters involved in launching and sustaining a comprehensive professional development project.

In this chapter, we explain what we mean by "accountability" and describe the mechanisms for being *held to account* in professional development. In our discussion of the what, the how, and the to whom of our accountability system, we get to the nuts-and-bolts of providing high-quality professional development. Although we discuss these practical matters in the context of the LS Project, the objectives, procedures, processes, and tools are applicable to other large-scale professional development efforts.

ACCOUNTABILITY IN PROFESSIONAL DEVELOPMENT

We, along with our readers, who have many years of experience in education, have witnessed an increased demand for accountability in schools and in higher education. The what, the how, and the to whom of accountability grows out of relationships among individuals' and institutions' conceptions of accountability *and* the internal and external systems in which accountability operates (Wagner, 1989). What *accountability* means, who is held to account, what data are included to establish accountability, how information is channeled and reported, and to whom the account is rendered are all functions of internal accountability (Abelmann & Elmore, 1999). These functions are also shaped by external accountability mechanisms, such as federal and state laws regarding testing and school-funding decisions tied to meeting annual progress benchmarks.

National, state, and local educational policies largely define what is meant by "accountability" for schools, teachers, and students. Schools are held accountable for student achievement; teachers are held accountable for delivering evidenced-based instruction that leads to high student achievement; and students are held accountable for meeting learning expectations. Standards of accrediting bodies—for example, the National Council for Accreditation of Teacher Education (NCATE) that has existed for 50 years and the newer Teacher Education Accreditation Council (TEAC)—hold higher education institutions accountable for providing individuals with the knowledge, skills, and dispositions to positively impact student learning. Although we have witnessed an increasing demand for accountability across educational arenas, professional development has largely escaped this demand due to a lack of formal policies and clear definitions of accountability.

Recently, however, three major thrusts in education have propelled a movement toward accountability in professional development. First, today we have a better understanding of how effective professional development should be designed and evaluated. Wilson and Berne (1999), for example, derived several themes from their examination of six exemplary cases of effective professional development. They defined *effective professional development* as inservice programs or activities that result in positive changes in teachers' professional knowledge. In the cases they investigated, several conditions existed to create communities of learners, which redefined teaching practice and sustained ongoing professional development. The professional development not only brought new content to the teachers but also engaged them in thinking about their own knowledge in relation to their students' knowledge. The professional development set up learning contexts that privileged teachers' interactions with each other, and thereby built trust while aiming for a professional discourse that included and did not avoid critique (Wilson & Berne, 1999, p. 195). In other words, the stance of "We're all in this together" was adopted.

More generally, a body of educational research has converged on many principles that guide the design of effective professional development (Ball & Cohen, 1999; Crockett, 2002; Goldenberg & Gallimore, 1991; Hawley & Valli, 1999; Richardson, 1994; Sparks, 2005; Wilson & Berne, 1999). These include:

- Substantive content that pushes for deeper understanding about teaching and learning that is essential.
- Participants have ample opportunity to discuss theory and research.
- The approach to professional learning is inquiry-based.
- Participants engage in collaborative problem solving around teaching and learning artifacts (e.g., lesson plans, student work samples, audio- and videotaped lessons).
- Problem-solving activity presses for analyzing, giving and receiving constructive feedback, and reflecting on one's own practice. In so doing, participants assume a critical stance toward their own practice.

A second thrust toward accountability in professional development is the use of research results by educators and policymakers alike to establish standards for high-quality professional development. Under the No Child Left Behind Act, the standards of high-quality professional development set up expectations for what states and schools should offer as professional learning opportunities to enhance teachers' learning and practice in ways that boost student achievement. Using these standards as guideposts, professional developers, policymakers, and stakeholders set criteria to monitor and evaluate their professional development programs and activities (e.g., Learning First Alliance, 2000; No Child Left Behind [U.S. Department of Education, 2001]; National Staff Development Council, 2001).

A third thrust for accountability in professional development is the heightened awareness of the cost of professional development as a major component of state budgets. As state officials prepare budgets for legislative approval, they are required to justify how dollars are spent for services in relation to the outcomes achieved. In other words, are the services cost effective? To answer this question, tracking records become increasingly important. These include numbers to show impact: how many (participants), how much (service), and how beneficial (to teachers and students)? The press for accountability in professional development is heightened as huge investments in resources to design and deliver professional development are made and extensive amounts of time and effort are given to inservice programs.

ACCOUNTABILITY IN THE LITERACY SPECIALIST PROJECT

At the outset of the LS Project, we knew that gathering evidence on the level of participation, service, and benefits was no small matter in this large-scale initiative. We also recognized that it was critical to know what we would be held accountable for, and to also put in place the appropriate mechanisms to systematically gather information to deliver a comprehensive and accurate account of the project to our state funders, participants, and stakeholders.

For what is the LS Project held accountable?, *How do we keep account?*, and *To whom do we account?* are questions we answer in this section. As we make explicit our conception of accountability and our tools and methods for getting the job done, we invite our readers to anticipate some answers to these questions in relation to how you are or could be held to account in your own professional development work (see Figure 7.1).

At the beginning of any teaching work, whether in classrooms, university courses, or professional development sessions, it is important to clearly articulate goals around a quality curriculum and to adhere to standards of practice

For what is the Literacy Specialist Project held accountable?	Accountability in the LS Project is for the wide dissemination of a high-quality professional development to K–3 teachers, monitoring its implementation across the state, and evaluating the effectiveness of what we do in relation to what we need to achieve: increase teacher knowledge about literacy teaching and improve teaching performance.
How do we keep account?	We use data collection tools and methods to monitor project participation, implementation, and learning. • Rosters of participation • Meeting schedules, agenda, and minutes • Memorandum of Understanding • Session Implementation Feedback, Evaluation, and Attendance forms • Teacher Knowledge pre- and postsurveys • Participants' Information Survey
To whom are we accountable?	We report to state funders, participants, and stakeholders.

FIGURE 7.1. Accountability tools and methods in the LS Project.

that will assure that learning takes place. Thinking about our teaching work on a large scale, such as in the LS Project, we understood the goal to be wide dissemination of knowledge, skills, and dispositions foundational to effective K–3 reading instruction, which, in turn, could lead to capacity building within schools for high-quality instruction. With this goal in mind, accountability in the LS Project is conceptualized as the wide dissemination of high-quality professional development to K–3 teachers, monitoring its implementation across the state, and evaluating the effectiveness of what we do in relation to what we need to achieve: increased teacher knowledge about literacy teaching and improved teaching performance. This conceptualization of accountability can apply to professional development in any content area and at any grade level. In essence, for professional developers and other educators as well, accountability is assuring something of substance to teach, monitoring how well it is taught, and evaluating whether or not the intended outcomes are reached.

Our broad conception of accountability is not fixed; we continually work to refine it as the project expands and we understand more about effective professional development and ways to measure effectiveness. Thus far, we include four objectives within our accountability framework. These objectives are not meant to depict a linear approach to accountability, one objective at a time; rather, these objectives are overlapping and integrated, such that one depends on the other to achieve the outcome of the professional development: increased teacher knowledge and improved teaching practice. Our four objectives include:

1. Meeting the goal of widely disseminating professional development to K–3 educators.
2. Achieving high standards of research-based professional development.
3. Assuring fidelity to the implementation design.
4. Evaluating the impact of the professional development on teacher knowledge and practice and ultimately student achievement.

Meeting the Goal

To meet the goal of widely disseminating professional development to K–3 educators, we first needed an effective system for recruiting the faculty and literacy specialists who could provide the professional development to all areas of the state. Second, we needed a systematic way to keep track of the participants across the networks.

System of Recruitment

Field Faculty. Our recruitment of reading faculty members from universities was simple and straightforward. The number and location of the faculty had to be based on the number of participating districts and schools within reasonable proximity to a university. In collaboration with the state project leaders, we communicated directly with faculty we knew through prior association and/or chairpersons at the prospective universities. We found that the reading faculty members were readily interested in developing collegial relationships and working in schools, especially since this is what most had been doing individually for some time at their own institutions. As we explained in Chapter 2, once the faculty members fully understood the goal and reached consensus on the core curriculum, they were quite willing to join the initiative. The possibilities for scholarship and state subgrants to the participating universities made the invitation even more attractive. Negotiating with their chairs or deans for course release was the challenge, given the limited number of full-time reading faculty already stretched too thinly at most of the institutions. The subgrants, however, made it feasible for the institutions to participate. The subgrants covered indirect costs to the university, salary, and fringes equivalent to a .25 full-time equivalent (FTE) courseload reduction each semester, and all expenses related to the project (e.g., travel, meeting expenses, professional development resources for the literacy specialists, supplies, copying, mailing).

Districts and Schools. As in many other states, the control over professional development dollars and activities in Ohio resides with the districts and schools, unless the school is in need of state intervention due to its continuous low academic performance. School leaders become aware of the initiative through various communications:

- The state may target schools for the project (as did Ohio under the Reading Excellence Act).
- Field faculty members contact local district personnel.
- Project participants spread the word through their own networks.
- Field faculty, literacy specialists, and state leaders present information about the project at various state, regional, and district meetings.

As soon as someone (e.g., faculty member, literacy specialist, district or school administrator, or teacher) contacts the project office, the recruitment process shifts into high gear. The project director or designated staff member follows up immediately with the interested party by sending an application packet and continuing the chain of communication until the district's or school's participation is confirmed. This process can take from 1 week to a few months, especially as the process gets underway in late spring and does not end until late September (see Figure 7.2).

We anticipate our participation level for the upcoming year by surveying the current participants each spring. Like the recruitment process, the retention process works much the same as a communication system that helps to assure

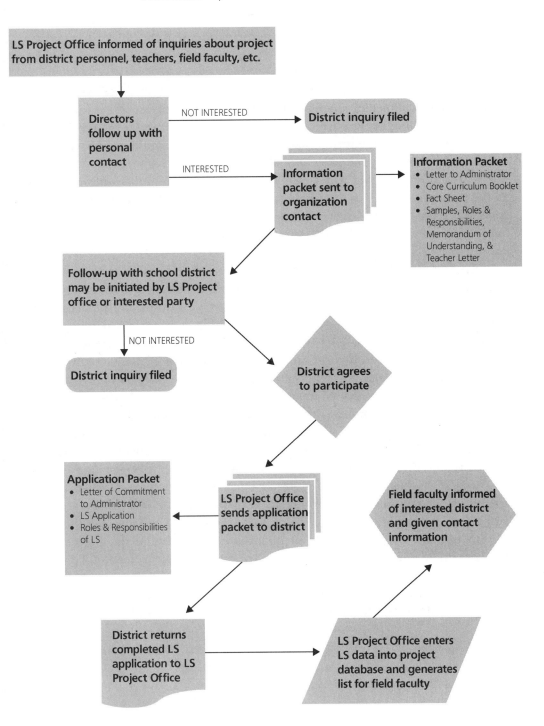

FIGURE 7.2. LS Project's recruitment process flowchart.

that we have an accurate record of our participation, that the database is current and accurate.

Literacy Specialists. Literacy specialists are district employees. The recommended qualifications for a person serving in this position are at least 3 years of successful teaching experience on a professional license and a master's degree with reading endorsement or a master's degree in reading education. A district administrator, typically the professional development or language arts coordinator, will identify a teacher who meets these qualifications and is willing to serve in the position. As soon as this person is on board, the field faculty member contacts the literacy specialist with information on the meeting schedule, place, times, and other logistical matters of getting started.

Teachers. The literacy specialists and the school or district administrator are responsible for recruiting teachers. Teacher participation is decided at the local level. The literacy specialists often come up with their own motivational perks to pique teachers' interest. Some will place flyers in teachers' mailboxes, make announcements at building-level teacher meetings, and even conduct a more formal PowerPoint presentation that overviews the project. Field faculty members or project staff may also meet with teacher groups to solicit their participation in the professional development. They underscore and explain the professional growth opportunities, appealing to teachers' interest in continuous learning and collaboration with colleagues. They also explain the university credit options and continuing education units that will help them meet state and district requirements for maintaining their teaching credentials (see Figure 7.3).

Sometimes this is not enough because teachers have to experience a bit of the professional development to buy in. Realizing this in our second year of the project, we created the Introduction Session for literacy specialists and field faculty to use in their orientations of potential participants in the project. The Introduction Session folder provides an overview of the project and the core

---

Professional Growth Opportunities
- Gain insights into literacy teaching performance
- Acquire professional materials and resources
- Experience satisfaction of professional learning
- Participate in efforts to inform literacy policy

Professional Development Incentives
- Support individual professional development plan
- Earn graduate credit (based on participating university offerings)

FIGURE 7.3. Opportunities and incentives.

curriculum, and involves the teachers in learning activities to whet their appetite for learning more. For example, in the Introduction Session problem-solving activity, the literacy specialist leads participants in reviewing the components and conceptual elements in the professional development content (what teachers need to know and be able to do in their overall teaching work) and the Ohio Academic Content Standards: K–12 English Language Arts (Ohio Department of Education, 2002) (what students need to know and be able to do). They then chart some of their responses to three questions: What do you already know about the concepts? What does the research say about these elements? Which of the English language arts standards is most relevant to the component? The substantive conversation in a collegial setting is usually enough to win over skeptics who ask "What's in it for me?" because the opening activity is relevant to what they need to know and do in their own teaching work.

Overall, the literacy specialists show a strong track record for recruiting their colleagues to participate in the project. Usually they get the expected number of teachers to volunteer. Across the networks, voluntary participation is the norm. Less frequently, administrators strongly encourage some teachers to participate because they see the need for them to do so. Those teachers have typically been resistant to all opportunities for professional development offered by the district.

System of Keeping Track and Assuring Accuracy

At the outset of the project, we carefully planned procedures for data collection to keep track of participation. We developed and disseminated user-friendly methods and tools for gathering and storing data collected on the number and demographics of the participants and their reasons for participation. To gather information systematically, we first designed tools in collaboration with the field faculty, defined a clear set of protocols for administration, and field-tested the tools with a few people in the networks. The informal trials gave us sufficient feedback to make final adjustments before disseminating the tools to the networks statewide.

Typically we rely on the networks to gather information. The field faculty members are the first line of data collection. They explain the data collection methods to the literacy specialists in their respective groups during monthly meetings. The literacy specialists, in turn, gather information from their teachers during part of a session. We provide postage-paid, preaddressed envelopes (from the project budget) to help assure easy return of the data to the project office within a specified time frame.

Gathering Data at the Beginning of the Year. At the outset of each year, we gather basic contact information on the literacy specialists and the teachers. Field faculty members submit rosters listing groups of literacy specialists in their region. Literacy specialists submit rosters of the participating teachers. In addition, all participants are required to sign a Memorandum of Understanding, which confirms their earnest intent to participate fully for the duration of the 15 sessions. We all establish our schedules for the year: field faculty meetings, field faculty and literacy specialists meetings, and literacy specialist–teacher sessions. The schedules for all the networks are forwarded to the project office and entered on a master calendar.

This information is continually updated throughout the year at field faculty meetings. The field faculty members maintain their rosters and continually verify them with the literacy specialists. They then report any changes to the project office. This system of checks and balances continues with the office personnel editing the rosters as needed and returning them to the field faculty member for confirmation. Although this is a mundane task, it is essential to keep track of participants and their comings and goings throughout a yearlong project. One of the ways to measure progress toward the goal of widely disseminating professional development is to know the number of teachers, literacy specialists, schools, and districts participating in the project each year.

Information that describes who the participants are is also helpful in meeting the goals of the professional development. For example, knowing the educational background of participants helps to define the audience. Therefore, in addition to keeping track of project rosters and schedules, we gather data on the literacy specialists through two surveys that are administered in the same meeting or session at the beginning of the project: the teacher Motivation to Participate Survey (Figure 7.4), and the demographic Participant Information Survey, which gathers information on the educational background, teaching experience, and professional development activity of the literacy specialists and teachers (Figure 7.5).

Because project participation is voluntary, the motivation survey helps us find out what motivates the teachers and other educators to get involved and make the yearlong commitment to the professional development. This 14-item survey asks participants to rate factors that they consider influences on their participation (e.g., improve teaching practice, acquire professional resources, earn college credit) on a Likert scale from 1 = little influence to 5 = great influence.

Gathering Data throughout the Year. Throughout the year, attendance is taken at meetings across the network. Records are submitted to the project office where data are analyzed to monitor increases and decreases in participation, to compare participation in various regions or school districts, and to track the number of years that teachers and literacy specialists participate.

Numbers related to attendance and participation are tallied and demographic information is compiled for quarterly reports to the state department of education. These data are used to document levels and types of participation each year, which help to justify ongoing state support.

Field Faculty Network in Literacy Education Project: Motivation to Participate Survey

Dear Participating Teacher,

As we try to extend and improve the program for next year, we need your help. In the case of this brief survey we are interested in the factors that influenced your decision to participate. Please take a few moments to recall your reasons for wanting to participate in the Literacy Specialist Project. Below you will find a list of possible factors followed by a five-point rating scale from *1=little influence (had little influence on my decision to participate)* to *5=great influence (had great influence on my decision to participate).* For each factor please circle the appropriate rating. We have also included spaces for you to add factors that may have influenced your decision. Please feel free to add such factors and circle the approrpriate rating for them as well. Finally, we have provided some space for you to write in any comments that you think would further explain your reasons for participating. Thank you for your cooperation.

Factors	Little Influence			Great Influence	
Learning new things	1	2	3	4	5
Improving your teaching	1	2	3	4	5
Discussions with other teachers	1	2	3	4	5
Opportunity for support from a literacy specialist	1	2	3	4	5
Content of sessions	1	2	3	4	5
Materials	1	2	3	4	5
Respect for your literacy specialist	1	2	3	4	5
District level encouragement	1	2	3	4	5
Building level encouragement					
Peer encouragement	1	2	3	4	5
Professional credential (endorsement)	1	2	3	4	5
Course credit					
Convenience	1	2	3	4	5
Financial reward	1	2	3	4	5
_____	1	2	3	4	5
_____	1	2	3	4	5

Comments: _____

FIGURE 7.4. Motivation to Participate Survey.

Field Faculty Network in Literacy Education Project
Participant Information Survey – K-3 Core Curriculum

Please take a few minutes to complete the following items. The information you provide will be summarized along with that of other participants to describe generally the educational background of participants in the K-3 Core Curriculum.

Participant's Name _____

School _____District_____

1 Current position _____

2 How many years have you been teaching children? _____

3 What is your gender? (Circle the number of your answer.) 1 Female   2 Male

4 What is your racial or ethnic identity? (Optional) (Circle one number.)

    1 Black/African American   2 White/European American   3 Hispanic/Latino
    4 Asian/Pacific Islander   5 Native American/Eskimo   6 Multiracial
    7 Other racial or ethnic group (Please specify group.) _____

5 Circle the number in front of your highest level of education. Write in the year you earned the degree.
    1 Bachelor's Degree _____   2 Master's Degree _____   3 Doctorate _____

6 Are you currently enrolled in a higher education program leading to an advanced degree? (Circle the number of your answer.)
    1 Yes   2 No
    If yes, what is the degree you are seeking? _____ What institution? _____

7 What activities do you engage in to advance your professional knowledge and skills in teaching literacy? (Check all that apply and circle the response indicating how often you engage in the activity.)

    ❏ Attend workshops, inservices, and other professional development activities offered locally:
      once a year   twice a year   three or more times a year

    ❏ Attend local, state, regional conferences:
      once a year   twice a year   three or more times a year

    ❏ Make a presentation at professional conferences:
      once a year   twice a year   three or more times a year

    ❏ Read professional magazines or journals:
      once a year   twice a year   three or more times a year

    ❏ Write articles for educational journals, magazines, and newsletters:
      once a year   twice a year   three or more times a year

Thank you for taking the time to provide this information!

FIGURE 7.5. Participant Information Survey.

Achieving High Standards of Research-Based Professional Development

As discussed in Chapter 2, the project centers on a research-based core curriculum, *Teaching Reading and Writing: A Core Curriculum for Educators* (Roskos, 2000). The document describes how the curriculum links research and practice and serves to create a shared knowledge base among teachers to improve student learning. The core curriculum identifies what teachers need to know and be able to do for effective literacy instruction, and it provides a conceptual framework designed to impact teaching and learning. How well the curriculum can support the participants in achieving the intended outcomes, in part, relies on how well the professional development is designed.

As a way to continually validate the professional development sessions that stem from the core curriculum, that is, to establish content validity, we pursue three courses of action: (1) ongoing review of literacy research and pedagogy, (2) content analysis of learning activities in the professional development sessions, and (3) alignment of the professional development with nationally recognized curricula, professional development standards, and the state's academic content standards.

Review of Current Literature

Each year we review current research from peer-reviewed journals to identify articles that relate to the session content and decide whether or not to substitute more current readings in the session supplements for the ones that we already include. We also take into account the feedback from the field faculty and literacy specialists on whether or not the readings are challenging for and meeting the needs and interests of the teachers throughout the state. The supplemental readings are a regular part of the monthly field faculty–literacy specialists meetings. The minutes from those meetings provide a valuable source for gathering information that contributes to our account of the quality of the professional development.

Content Analyses of Learning Activities

To closely examine how well the *Field Work* activities meet the professional learning goals of the core curriculum, we, along with several members of the field faculty, analyzed the problem-solving activities according to the four categories of the knowledge dimension (factual, conceptual, procedural, and metacognitive) and the six categories (remember, understand, apply, analyze, evaluate, and create) of cognitive processes of Bloom's Taxonomy—Revised (Krathwohl, 2002). The analysis showed that across all 15 sessions the *Field Work* activities pressed for higher-level thinking across the knowledge domains (see Figure 7.6).

	Factual Knowledge						Conceptual Knowledge						Procedural Knowledge						Metacognitive Knowledge					
	remember	understand	apply	analyze	evaluate	create	remember	understand	apply	analyze	evaluate	create	remember	understand	apply	analyze	evaluate	create	remember	understand	apply	analyze	evaluate	create
Session 1										x	x	x			x x x			x						
Session 2	x	x x								x	x	x x			x			x x						
Session 3		x							x		x x		x		x									
Session 4										x	x x		x									x	x	
Session 5	x	x						x		x x	x x	x			x		x	x					x x	
Session 6		x x x						x x		x			x x	x x										
Session 7		x									x x x	x	x											
Session 8	x x										x x	x												
Session 9										x	x x x	x	x	x		x	x					x	x	
Session 10										x	x x x	x	x	x		x	x					x	x	
Session 11										x	x x x	x	x	x		x	x					x	x	
Session 12										x	x x x	x	x	x		x	x					x	x	
Session 13										x x	x x		x			x	x							
Session 14								x			x x	x	x		x			x					x	
Session 15												x	x		x			x					x	

FIGURE 7.6. Analysis of Field Work using Bloom's Taxonomy—Revised (Krathwohl, 2002).

This type of close analysis not only allowed us to assess the content validity of the professional development but it also gave us a window into which problem-solving and *Field Work* activities we needed to improve in order to better support teachers in achieving the increased-knowledge outcome of the professional development.

Alignment of the Professional Development

In our third level of assessing content validity of the professional development, we looked at alignment of the core curriculum professional development with that described in (1) a nationally recognized professional development curriculum (Moats, 2002), (2) professional development standards, and (3) Ohio's English language arts standards. For these analyses, we created matrixes to help us make explicit the alignment. As with the other means for addressing the what of accountability, we have used the results to strengthen and refine the professional development to better meet the intended outcomes of the professional development: increased teacher knowledge and improved practice.

Alignment with Professional Development Curriculum. We compared the professional development outlined in the 15-session core curriculum with the one described in *A Blueprint for Professional Development for Teachers of Reading: Knowledge, Skills, and Learning Activities* (Moats, 2002). The blueprint identifies the knowledge and skills teachers need in order to understand and implement scientifically based reading instruction and suggests types of professional development activities teachers need in order to improve their instruction. We found that both the blueprint and the core curriculum address the knowledge teachers need in order to understand reading instruction, the skills teachers need in order to teach reading well, and the professional learning activities needed to examine and reflect on the practice of teaching reading. We found that major areas of focus for teaching reading (e.g., text comprehension, phonemic awareness, letter knowledge) are closely aligned, and that components present in one curriculum are also present in the other. For example, when addressing text comprehension, Moats includes "Understand comprehension monitoring strategies commonly used by good readers." Our alignment shows that the core curriculum addresses text comprehension-monitoring strategies in Session 11 with whole-group discussion of comprehension strategy instruction, small-group activities examining features of comprehension lessons, and supplemental readings (Figure 7.7). This type of scrutiny of the professional development sessions proved useful for validating the key concepts taught in the core curriculum, taking into account if and how to make modifications in the materials, and articulating how the core curriculum aligned with a nationally validated professional development curriculum in literacy.

Moats	Core Curriculum Session	Examples from Materials and Readings
Understand comprehension monitoring strategies commonly used by good readers.	Teaching about comprehension	**Activities:** Examination of instructional features of comprehension lessons. **Graphic:** Comprehension Strategies Worth Teaching **Transparencies:** Teaching comprehension strategies and techniques **Readings:** Beck, I., McKeown, M., Hamilton, R., & Kucan, L. (1998). Getting at the meaning: How to help students unpack difficult text. *American Educator, Spring/Summer,* 66–77.
Differentiate among strategies that are appropriate before, during, and after reading.	Teaching about comprehension	**Activities:** Examination of instructional features of comprehension lessons. **Graphic:** Comprehension Strategies Worth Teaching **Transparencies:** Teaching comprehension strategies and techniques **Readings:** Tower, C. (2000). Questions that matter: Preparing elementary students for the inquiry process. *The Reading Teacher, 53,* 550–557.
Contrast the characteristics of major text genres, including narration, exposition, and argumentation.	Knowing about English language	**Activities:** Determining text structure and planning teaching of text structure. **Graphic:** Samples of text structure and text cues **Transparencies:** Text structures **Readings:** Staal, L. (2000). The story face: An adaption of story mapping that incorporates visualization and discovery learning to enhance reading and writing. *The Reading Teacher, 54,* 27–31.
Identify text structure and syntax (phrases, clauses, sentences, paragraphs, and "academic language") that could be a source of miscomprehension.	Knowing about English language Teaching about comprehension	**Activities:** Determining text structure and planning teaching of text structure. **Graphic:** Samples of text structure and text cues **Transparencies:** Text structures **Readings:** Beck, I., McKeown, M., Hamilton, R., & Kucan, L. (1998). Getting at the meaning: How to help students unpack difficult text. *American Educator, Spring/Summer,* 66–77.
Understand the similiarities and differences between written composition and text comprehension, and the usefulness of writing in building comprehension.	Knowing about literacy processes Teaching writing	**Activities:** Examination of writing samples and analysis of writing instruction **Graphic:** The Composing Process **Readings:** Butler, K., & Turbill, J. (1984). The reading–writing process. In *Towards a reading-writing classroom* (pp. 11–20). Portsmouth, NH: Heinemann. Button, K., Johnson, J., Furgerson, P. (1999). Interactive writing in a primary classroom. In *Reading Research Anthology: The why? of reading instruction* (pp. 200–215). Novato, CA: Arena Press.

FIGURE 7.7. Core curriculum session content on text comprehension aligned with *A Blueprint for Professional Development for Teachers of Reading: Knowledge, Skills, and Learning Activities* (Moats, 2002).

Alignment with Ohio Academic Content Standards: K–12 English Language Arts. The core curriculum conceptual elements discussed in Chapter 2 were analyzed to determine the connections between what teachers need to know, as stated in the core curriculum, and what students need to know, as outlined in the English language arts standards. Our analysis confirmed a high degree of overlap between the core curriculum conceptual elements and the English language arts standards for grades K–3. The core curriculum professional development sessions for teachers include literacy content and teaching concepts aligned with the 44 benchmarks for the English arts standards. We found strong links across all four domains. The core curriculum specifically addresses K–3 benchmarks for the English language arts standards with a few exceptions: (1) author's word choices and influences on the reader, (2) teaching the use of resources for determining word meaning and pronunciation, and (3) following multistep directions.

Alignment with Professional Development Principles. We think that any professional development should align with research-based principles. In the LS Project, we aligned the professional development with the No Child Left Behind Act definition of high-quality professional development (U.S. Department of Education, 2001) and 10 research-based principles (Ball & Cohen, 1999; Hawley & Valli, 1999; Sykes, 1999; Wilson & Berne, 1999). We carried out this process independently, then compared our evidence in order to establish interrater agreement. As our alignment matrix (Figure 7.8) shows, the LS Project adequately meets 10 research-based principles of high-quality professional development.

Assuring Fidelity in the Implementation

When disseminating a single professional development model to multiple sites, it is important to ensure fidelity of implementation (Borko, 2004). Given that we designed the session structure and the learning activities based on tenets that undergird effective professional development approaches, we wanted to know which session structural elements and materials the literacy specialists implemented as designed, and which ones they modified or omitted, and their reasons for doing so. We put in place a system for keeping track of the implementation in these ways.

During their first meeting of the school year, field faculty members distribute record-keeping folders to their literacy specialists. Record-keeping folders contain instructions and a set of implementation feedback forms for all core curriculum sessions (see example in Figure 7.9). Each feedback form lists the session structure and materials as they are identified in each of the session folders.

Following a session, the literacy specialists record "how" they used the session parts (e.g., *Before, During, After*) and the materials to conduct the session. They mark on the implementation feedback form which parts and materials they

1 Built around Ongoing Collaboration
  - The network structure brings together university faculty, teachers, literacy specialists, and school district administrators around a common goal.
  - Literacy specialists engage teachers in discussions and small-group activities during 15 site-based sessions that take place throughout the school year.
  - Schoolwide involvement helps develop a learning community.

2 Supported by Skillful Leadership
  - Administrators, literacy specialists, and teachers sign a Memorandum of Understanding declaring their commitment to the professional development.
  - Practical resources are provided, including:
    - Core Curriculum for educators
    - Professional development tools and materials for each session
    - Professional books and videos.

3 Continuous and Reflective
  - Participants learn through 15 2–3 hour sessions that are presented over the school year.
  - Participants discuss literacy topics and engage in problem-solving activities during each session.
  - Participants apply new learning to their own teaching through personal reflection and field work activities.
  - Coaching is integral to the teaching–learning process.

4 Based on Student Data
  - Session activities and field work experiences provide multiple opportunities for teachers to collect, analyze, and interpret student data in order to monitor progress and plan instruction.

5 Designed and Planned by and for Educators
  - Small-group problem-solving and field work activities center on classroom practice.
  - Presentation and discussion of research develops understanding of literacy content and teaching.
  - Session activities and resources support clearly stated professional learning goals.

6 Aligned with Comprehensive Continuous Improvement Plan
  - Standards are embedded in the professional learning goals of all sessions. Teachers explore the English language arts standards, benchmarks, and indicators; and plan and implement standards-based instruction.

7 Evaluated from Multiple Perspectives
  - Data on the session implementation are gathered using multiple tools. Pre- and post-surveys examine teacher learning.
  - Literacy specialists, who meet regularly with reading faculty from Ohio colleges and universities, deliver core curriculum content. Literacy specialists participate in and provide professional development in SBRR, and disseminate SBRR resources.

8 Focused on Student Achievement
  - The core curriculum content is aligned with the English language arts standards to demonstrate the connection between teacher knowledge and student learning.
  - The aim of the core curriculum is to develop an understanding of reading and writing to improve teaching. Sessions focus on collecting student data to provide assessment-based instruction and intervention. The Assess–Plan–Teach Instructional Cycle is embedded in each session.

9 Designed to Promote Cultural Competency
  - Sessions on literacy development and literacy processes specifically address the characteristics of diverse learners.
  - Participants gain knowledge of multiple assessment tools and instructional strategies to meet the needs of diverse learners.

10 Based on Research
  - Participants examine SBRR content and instruction and apply effective strategies to their standards-based lesson plans that focus on the five essential components of reading instruction, oral language, and writing.
  - Participants examine components of effective classroom instruction during sessions and follow through with planning, implementing, and self-analyzing their own instruction.

FIGURE 7.8. Core curriculum alignment with 10 principles of high-quality professional development.

Directions: Please check (✓) the column that best describes your implementation of each session component. Forward this completed form to your field faculty as soon as possible.	Used as published (Made no changes.)	Omitted (Did not use.)	Modified (Changed in some way.)	Comments and/or description of changes. Use additional pages as needed. Attach copies of other materials used.
Background Information				
Professional Learning Goals				
Vocabulary				
Bright Starters				
Kit Materials				
Local Materials Reading/Writing Samples				
Ohio K-12 ELA Standards				
Before: **Share-Introduce-Explain**				
T1.1 The Diagnostic Process				
T1.2-1.4 Developmental Continuum				
T1.5-1.7 Emergent Samples				
T1.8 Analyzing Emergent Writing				
During: **Organize-Do-Record**				
A1.1 Activity				
A1.2-1.4 Early/Beginning Samples				
A1.5-1.7 Transitional Samples				
A1.8-1.10 Intermediate/Advanced Samples				
Bookshelf				
After: **Present-Discuss-Summarize**				
Worth a Look				
Reflection				
Field Work				
FW1.1 Literacy Development				
Making Connections				
Coming Up				
Supplemental Readings (Check cell appropriate columns to indicate use of readings.)	Studied	Copied for teachers.	Integraged into session.	Comments
Shaywitz, B., et al.				
Bear, D.				

Note: T=Transparency; A=Activity page; FW=Field Work. For example, T1.8 refers to the 8th transparency in Session 1; A1.4 refers to the 4th activity page in Session 1; FW1.1 refers to the 1st field work page in Session 1.

FIGURE 7.9. Session 1 implementation feedback form.

used as designed, modified, or omitted. If the literacy specialists make any modifications or omissions, they are asked to comment on those changes and attach any copies of other materials they used or substituted for the ones provided with the session. Literacy specialists then submit the implementation feedback forms to the field faculty members, who review the responses before forwarding the forms to the project office. The data are analyzed for the purpose of assessing the fidelity of the core curriculum implementation and for formative evaluation to make instructional improvements.

Evaluating Outcomes of Professional Development

This last objective to meet in our accountability system gets to the intended outcomes in relation to the goal of the LS Project: to deepen understanding of literacy pedagogy. To demonstrate that the goal was met, we needed to assess changes in teacher's knowledge and practice. Although there is still much to learn about what makes professional development effective, the extant research confirms that we need much more than one-shot workshops or a patchwork of sporadic, random, decontextualized opportunities (Wilson & Berne, 1999, p. 174). Throughout this book, we have demonstrated that the LS project, unlike traditional approaches, is yearlong, substantive, inquiry-based, and connected to everyday practice. These elements support its potential for making a positive difference in teachers' knowledge and skills. Although it was no easy matter to measure teacher learning and changes in teacher practice, it was essential to begin to evaluate how well we were meeting these intended outcomes of the professional development model.

To assess change in teachers' knowledge, we developed a 24-item survey of teachers' self-perceptions of literacy teaching and learning based on the key concepts taught in the core curriculum. The teachers responded to theoretical and research statements, which we constructed from text in the session materials. The participants read each statement and then marked one response for each item. Figure 7.10 shows sample items from the survey.

Each year we administer the survey at the beginning and end of the year to all participating teachers. A comparison of the pre- and postscores provides a measure of change in teachers' self-perceptions of their knowledge, a proxy for teacher learning.

We also developed ways to examine the relationship between participation in the professional development and teachers' practice. Unlike the teachers' knowledge survey that we administered statewide, we analyzed this relationship on a much smaller scale due to limited financial and human resources. We look at the connections between participation and practice in different ways.

In addition to conducting their monthly all-day meetings with the literacy specialists, field faculty members conduct at least one observation of their literacy specialists' professional development sessions. They follow up with an interview that probes their understanding of how well the session was implemented,

Literacy Specialist Project
_____

Core Curriculum Concepts Survey

PURPOSE: To gather information about teacher understandings related to literacy instruction. The information will be used as part of a larger study of the Literacy Specialist Project.

Directions: Please respond carefully to the following questions that inquire about teaching reading and writing in your classroom and/or school. This survey should take approximately 30 minutes to complete. Submit your completed survey to the literacy specialist. (If you are an administrator, complete items 1 – 11 only.)

PROFESSIONAL BACKGROUND
[In this section of the survey, teachers are asked to complete questions related to their background.]

Sample questions:
2. Circle the number in front of **each education degree** you hold. Write in parentheses the year you earned each degree.
   1. Bachelor's (_____) 2. Master's (_____) 3. Specialist (_____) 4. Doctorate (_____)

4. How many **total years** have you spent as an elementary teacher? Write 0 if this is your first year of teaching.
   _____ years

TEACHER UNDERSTANDINGS ABOUT LITERACY
[In this section, teachers are asked to circle the response that best describes their understanding of each concept.]

Sample questions:
14. Through the process of talking and interacting with others, children build up practical knowledge of their inherited language systems.
    1. I **understand** this statement **thoroughly and could lead a discussion** on the topic.
    2. I **understand** this statement **and could explain** it to a colleague.
    3. I **understand** this statement **but not well enough to explain** it to a colleague.
    4. I am **somewhat familiar** with this statement **but could not explain** it to a colleague.
    5. I **do not understand** this statement at all.

15. The alphabetic principle refers to the sound units in oral language, which are associated with letter units of the written alphabet.
    1. I **understand** this statement **thoroughly and could lead a discussion** on the topic.
    2. I **understand** this statement **and could explain** it to a colleague.
    3. I **understand** this statement **but not well enough to explain** it to a colleague.
    4. I am **somewhat familiar** with this statement **but could not explain** it to a colleague.
    5. I **do not understand** this statement at all.

23. Expectations in the form of standards, competencies, and curricular outcomes inform and shape literacy teaching practice.
    1. I **understand** this statement **thoroughly and could lead a discussion** on the topic.
    2. I **understand** this statement and **could explain it** to a colleague.
    3. I **understand** this statement **but not well enough to explain** it to a colleague.
    4. I am **somewhat familiar** with this statement **but could not explain** it to a colleague.
    5. I **do not understand** this statement at all.

34. The process of interpreting observational data involves identifying the child's strengths and needs by comparing what the child knows to what the child needs to know to advance as a reader and writer.
    1. I **understand** this statement **thoroughly and could lead a discussion** on the topic.
    2. I **understand** this statement **and could explain it** to a colleague.
    3. I **understand** this statement **but not well enough to explain** it to a colleague.
    4. I am **somewhat familiar** with this statement **but could not explain it** to a colleague.
    5. I **do not understand** this statement at all

Thank you for taking time to complete this survey.

FIGURE 7.10. Sample of Core Curriculum Concepts Survey.

their preparation activities, and their perceptions of the teachers' participation and learning. These data are used by field faculty to improve their professional development for literacy specialists, which involves everything from literacy content to teaching adults to managing the presentation of materials and content, time, and so on. The field faculty members are held accountable for communicating this information to the project director as another mechanism for improving the quality of the professional development program.

We also assess how well teachers transfer the concepts taught in the professional session to their practice. The field faculty members collect samples of teachers' *Field Work* to identify links between the professional development and classroom practice. We look for evidence of the extent to which the procedures are implemented and evidence of understanding, misunderstanding, or partial understanding of concepts included in the session content and activities. We recognize that the literacy specialists are the communicators of the *Field Work*, and therefore influence what and how the teachers take forth key concepts from the session and apply them to their own practice. A close analysis of these teachers' work samples, like student work samples, provides a window into how well the concepts and skills taught are promoting more skilled teaching. Like the observations and interviews, the *Field Work*, or applications to practice activities, provides rich data sources for documenting accountability for providing professional development that leads to improved practice.

We also assess change in participants' practice more directly by analyzing the data collected from literacy specialist and teacher coaching conversations. In Chapter 6, we zoomed in on a literacy specialist–teacher coaching conversation centered on carrying out *Field Work* in the teaching domain. Recall that the Teacher Learning Instrument was used to engage them in a set of processes beginning with planning and moving into teaching, and then analyzing, interpreting, and reflecting on teaching. After three cycles of this process, we observed that the teacher became more intentional and precise in her teaching as she paid closer attention to her students' performance. In these close-ups of instruction that stem directly from the session to the classroom we see the best evidence of the professional development leading to desirable changes in practice. (We have also researched the influence of professional development on teacher knowledge and practice. This discussion we reserve for Chapter 8.)

The mechanisms that we put in place in our accountability system may be adapted to other professional development initiatives. Put simply, accountability in professional development begins with having something to be accountable for, that is, delivery of substantive content to a group of educators for a specified goal related to teaching and learning. Next, the content validity of the curriculum needs to be established, its implementation tracked, its progress monitored, and its outcomes assessed. To do this in earnest requires a systematic approach in planning, devising methods and processes, and communicating regularly with participants and stakeholders.

OTHER PRACTICAL MATTERS

Managing a large-scale professional development effort requires attention to the practical matters of communicating to multiple audiences and committing resources. Through this discussion, we include details that we think will be useful in planning and disseminating professional development in a variety of contexts.

We communicate project information in a variety of ways to multiple audiences, including policymakers and stakeholders, such as the state department of education officials, school district administrators, school principals, literacy specialists, teachers, and local communities. Communication about the LS Project is critical to the effectiveness of this widespread project. The responsibility for communicating the LS Project's goals extends to all involved in the project.

A great deal of thought and resources go into developing materials and methods for communicating about the project's goals, project events, and the core curriculum. Information brochures, newsletters, reports, letters, notes, and e-mails are sent regularly to keep individuals abreast of project activities. In addition, the LS Project maintains a website designed to provide information to an even larger audience and to serve as a resource on literacy issues. We often make presentations at literacy conferences and meetings and visit state school districts to explain the LS Project.

The professional development network provides the structure for communicating among the many individuals and institutions involved in the LS Project. The field faculty and the project director meet monthly to review project goals and materials, plan professional development activities, and share news from their designated regions throughout the state. Communication continues when field faculty members meet monthly with the literacy specialists in their regions to introduce core curriculum materials, discuss project goals, and share areas of interest and concern within their regional school districts.

Communication methods must be accurate and must effectively convey the messages. Much of the communication involved in achieving project goals originates in the LS Project Office where a staff of professionals coordinates the production and dissemination of LS Project materials and manages the administrative aspects of the project. Regular staff meetings provide opportunities for communication around project goals and activities. Staff pays a great deal of attention to the accuracy of materials and the efficiency of communication channels.

It goes without saying that a project of this magnitude requires resources: human, time and space, and financial. All are essential to the management of a large-scale project. The magnitude of this project is apparent when you begin to envision the people involved in making it happen.

First and foremost are the people who make sure that high-quality professional development takes place on a day-to-day basis throughout the state: the field faculty, literacy specialists, school administrators, and teachers. Each person contributes unique qualities to his or her aspect of the project and its goal of improving teaching practice and student learning.

In addition to the university field faculty, literacy specialists, administrators, and teachers who are directly involved in the professional development activities, the LS Project employs a host of behind-the-scenes administrators, technicians, and consultants who assure smooth day-to-day operations.

Critical to the commitment of human, time, and space resources is the ability to establish funds to pay for these resources. While funds to manage the LS Project are provided by the State of Ohio, school districts find it necessary to be creative as they find funding from other sources, such as Title I, state literacy improvement grants, business partnerships, and PTA/PTO grants.

CLOSING

To reach the goal of widely disseminating a core curriculum to K–3 teachers throughout a state, we, along with our colleagues and state and school partners, established an infrastructure consisting of local networks of field faculty, literacy specialists, and teachers. This network system sets in motion the distribution of a research-based professional development model. Accountability for this work is achieved by identifying the goals for a large-scale professional development initiative and setting high expectations for a core curriculum designed around research-based principles. To achieve the intended learning outcomes—increased knowledge and improved teaching practice—the LS Project relies on an accountability system that includes systematic data gathering, an analyzing and reporting mechanism, and a continuous feedback loop from its stakeholders. LS Project leaders, faculty, and literacy specialists must be alert to the quality of curriculum implementation. They need to efficiently manage project funds, clearly communicate project goals, and accurately monitor project progress. As a result, they are accountable and hold themselves to high standards of professional development for educators.

In Chapter 8, we report findings from the LS Project research that tie closely to the accountability system. The research questions are derived from the intended outcomes of the project. We report on participants' motivation, fidelity of implementation, and knowledge and practice outcomes. The most difficult challenge of accountability in professional development is demonstrating the relationship between professional development and student achievement. The LS Project has not yet been able to demonstrate this relationship on a large scale. However, in Chapter 8, we present findings from cases that demonstrate the close relationships between professional development participation and student learning.

CHAPTER 8

Research on the Model

| Designing Research | Literacy Specialist Project Studies | Research We Need |

As a new field faculty member, I was struck by the power and possibilities for these professional development sessions to effect change. Like the proverbial stone thrown into a pond, we never know where or how far the ripples may take us when teachers examine their own practice (assess), make changes in their practice (plan), and voice what they have learned with others (teach).

—*The LS Exchange* (Vol. 18, p. 4, 2004)

All of us who are involved in professional development in one way or another realize the need for accountability and for evaluating how well our project's intended goals are being met. In Chapter 7, we explained the importance of accountability and provided many details about how to plan for and keep track of information that will help with answering questions directly related to the goals and outcomes of professional development. But beyond evaluation, it is also important to engage in systematic inquiry centered on key questions that will extend what we already know about professional development and potentially benefit the larger educational community.

In the LS Project, we conducted research on several aspects of this large-scale professional development initiative. We explored why teachers are willing to participate in a yearlong period of professional development. We examined the extent and quality of implementation. We also recognized that the goals of professional development are to increase knowledge and improve skills, and that assessing these goals would afford an opportunity to develop new, much-needed tools for doing so. Perhaps the most pressing research need and perhaps the most difficult need to fill is examining the connection between professional development and student achievement. Although the LS Project has not yet been able to demonstrate this relationship on a large scale, we have been able to examine this question on a small scale through case studies of literacy specialists coaching teachers toward more skilled teaching.

In this final chapter in our account of the LS Project, we describe our research in the project and how it not only intersects with the goals of the accountability system and the intended outcomes of the project, but also goes beyond these evaluation purposes. In this chapter, we describe our research and explain what our colleagues and we have learned about professional development through an examination of this wide-scale literacy initiative to improve K–3 reading and writing instruction. We also discuss the implications of this research and what further research is needed to design, implement, and evaluate effective professional development.

This chapter has two main sections. In the first section, we describe the research we have conducted over the first 3 years of the project. We present the major questions that drove our early investigations, report findings in relation to those overarching questions, and discuss some of the limitations of the research conducted thus far. In the second section, we delineate our next steps in pursuing research on the LS Project in particular, and, in the more general sense, we extend our thinking to issues in professional development that warrant further investigation, such as changing roles, conditions that support and constrain professional development, cost-effectiveness, and the growing role of technology.

DESIGNING RESEARCH

Research is an ongoing effort in the LS Project, one that we enjoy as a collaborative effort with our field faculty and literacy specialists. At the outset of the project, we carved an agenda that aimed to contribute to the growing body of research on professional development and also to inform stakeholders and policymakers about the efficacy of this large-scale literacy initiative in Ohio.

Theoretical and Research Perspectives

In constructing our research agenda for the LS Project, we grounded our work in sociocultural learning theories and current professional development research. Sociocultural theory deeply rooted in Vygotskian ideas (Vygotsky, 1978) of knowledgeable and skillful others serving as powerful mediators of learning provides a useful lens for exploring the adult learning contexts of professional development in the LS Project. Roland Tharp and Ronald Gallimore (1988) articulate and explain this sociocultural perspective in their 10-year study of instructional change in the Kamehameha Project (KEEP) in Hawaiian schools. Their research has guided the work of the LS Project and other school reform efforts today (e.g., Saunders & Goldenberg, 1996). Their idea of learning in schools stems from Vygotsky's "zone of proximal development" (ZPD), the contrast between what an individual can do with support from the environment, from others, and from the self, and what the individual can do independently. The ZPD, according to Tharp and Gallimore (1988), applies not only to children but also to the adults in the school setting. Just as a teacher's skillfully employed teaching actions carried out in the ZPD serve as a scaffold that supports a child's movement toward independent performance, a literacy specialist, a principal, or another teacher can scaffold other adults' learning and performance.

Tharp and Gallimore (1988) describe settings in which learning occurs as contexts of assisted performance, or *activity settings*. In these settings, people intentionally come together in designated places and interact in cultural ways to achieve a shared goal. An analysis of activity settings can reveal the physical resources (e.g., space, time, and objects), social resources (e.g., teachers, literacy specialists, and field faculty), and the relationships among them that assist people in achieving a shared goal. The professional development settings in the LS Project are activity settings. The common goal is to learn more about literacy teaching and to use that knowledge to improve practice. Although teachers learn in many different contexts of practice—for example, in on-the-run conversations with colleagues, in classrooms while teaching children, and in professional development contexts in and out of school settings (Putnam & Borko, 2000)—the networks of the LS Project professional development create intentional settings for colleagues to gather around the common goal of learning new content and skills to improve reading and writing instruction. Thus, a sociocultural lens is useful for examining the professional development in the LS Project as a context that supports professional learning.

Research on effective professional development further undergirds our studies of the LS Project. Our examination of current research has led us to recognize the attributes or components of professional development that make it effective. We outlined these attributes in Chapter 7. Essentially, critical elements of effective professional development (e.g., Ball & Cohen, 1999; Crockett, 2002; Hawley & Valli, 1999; Richardson, 1994) include (1) substantive content that pushes for deeper understanding about teaching and learning; (2) ample opportunity for participants to discuss theory and research; (3) an inquiry approach to professional learning that engages processes of analysis, giving and receiving constructive feedback, and reflection; and (4) collaborative problem solving around teaching and learning artifacts.

The influence of professional development on teacher practice has not been extensively researched (see Wilson & Berne, 1999). Contributing to a growing body of teacher research, studies have been conducted on how teachers learn and what factors are essential in supporting their learning. Some research has focused on inquiry-based tools that can be used for structured and systematic guidance, dialogue, and support for teacher reflection. Such research may be vital in discovering more about how teachers learn and the essential factors in their learning. Richardson's (1994) practical inquiry approach to professional development, for example, serves the dual purpose of deepening our understanding of reading pedagogy and achieving skillful teaching performance. Outside of literacy teaching—in mathematics education, for example—there is evidence that teachers' examination of student performance creates a "problem" to be solved that may lead to better lesson planning and implementation (Crockett, 2002). The literacy-teaching field needs various tools that promote teacher reflection and hold promise for increasing teacher expertise.

Planning the Research Agenda

In our construction of the core curriculum and its derived 15 professional development sessions, we were intentional about including research-based elements in the design of the professional development. We also realized that without a systematic inquiry, we would not know the extent to which the professional development would be implemented and which components would emerge as most salient from the literacy specialists' and teachers' perspectives. Further, to determine the viability of this emergent model of professional development for wider dissemination, we needed to identify critical processes in the implementation and how participation influenced teachers' knowledge and practice.

Given our theoretical stance, professional development research helped us to formulate our agenda in the LS Project. It made sense for us to start out by asking four basic questions about the implementation and the influence of professional development on teachers' knowledge and practice:

- Why do teachers and other educators participate in the LS Project?
- What is the fidelity of implementation to the professional development according to its design?
- What is the influence of the professional development on teachers' knowledge?
- What is the influence of the professional development on teachers' practice?

These questions build on one another, forming an integrated inquiry plan for conducting a systematic evaluation of professional development and for potentially contributing to a growing body of research on professional development models. We use the findings for both formative and summative evaluation purposes and also as the basis for pushing our research agenda forward.

- *Why do teachers and other educators participate in the LS Project?* We wondered, considering that project participation is voluntary, what motivated the teachers and other educators to get involved and make a yearlong commitment to the professional development. Motivation for learning is as important as the content to be learned and influences how much and how well teachers take hold of new ideas and apply them to their own practice. Motivation also affects how much time and effort people are willing to devote to learning (Bransford et al., 2000), especially when the opportunity demands even more of these investments beyond the already long and packed workday. Finding out early in the implementation what matters to teachers in signing on to a yearlong professional development project would help us to know how to sustain their motivation throughout the year and, even beyond 1 year, of professional development.

- *What is the fidelity of implementation to the professional development according to its design?* Among many questions to address regarding professional development implementation, fidelity is an important one to answer when disseminating a single professional development model in multiple sites (Borko, 2004). From a sociocultural perspective, Borko explains current trends in research on teacher professional development as three phases of research activity that examine four key elements of a professional development system: the professional development program, the teachers as learners, the professional developer who guides and assists teachers as they construct new knowledge and change their practice, and the context in which the professional development occurs. Phase 1 activities focus on an individual program at a single site. The researchers study the program, the teachers as learners, and the relationship between these two elements. In Phase 2, the researchers study a single professional development program implemented at more than one site by more than one professional developer. They explore the relationship among the facilitators, the program, and the teachers as learners. In Phase 3, the research questions broaden to compare multiple professional development programs, each enacted at multiple sites.

Our research on core curriculum professional development edges toward Phase 2. The core curriculum is one professional development model implemented by multiple providers at multiple sites. A research question to address in this phase is whether or not the different professional development providers can enact a professional development program with a similar degree of integrity in different settings. More specifically, given that we designed the session structure and the learning activities based on principles of effective professional development approaches, we wanted to find out which session components the literacy specialists implemented as designed, which ones they modified or omitted, and their reasons for doing so.

These last two questions get to the intended outcomes of the professional development: increased literacy content knowledge and improved teaching practice.

- *What is the influence of the professional development on teachers' knowledge?*
- *What is the influence of the professional development on teachers' practice?*

There were no easy-to-fit tools for assessing teacher learning and practice in this project. Thus, we had an opportunity to develop and pilot new instruments, and thereby to help address the need for valid and reliable instruments in professional development.

LITERACY SPECIALIST PROJECT STUDIES

We conducted both project-wide and small-scale studies in the LS Project to address our four research questions. We addressed questions 1 and 2 through the Teacher Motivation Study and the Fidelity of Implementation Study. We addressed questions 3 and 4 through the Change in Teacher Knowledge Study and the Change in Teacher Practice Study.

We used a variety of methods and tools to collect data from the LS Project participants, depending on our purpose and time, fiscal resources, and human resources. Figure 8.1 outlines the research design for the four LS Project studies.

We primarily used surveys for collecting data across the project. The surveys were typically administered through the networks, that is, the field faculty gathered data from the literacy specialists, who, in turn, gathered information from the teachers and the other educators (e.g., principals, language arts coordinators, paraprofessionals) who participated in the professional development. On a much smaller scale, we gathered more in-depth information from participants through observations, interviews, and the Teacher Learning Instrument (TLI). (Refer to Chapter 6 for a full description of the TLI.) We describe these methods in more detail in our report on each of the studies.

The participants in the studies included literacy specialists and teachers. Over the first 3 years, the LS Project brought together 14 field faculty members from 10 universities, 353 literacy specialists, and 2,059 teachers in 122 school districts throughout the state. Tables 8.1 and 8.2 show the demographics of par-

	Research Question	Source	Method	Time Frame
TEACHER MOTIVATION STUDY	Why do teachers and other educators participate in the Literacy Specialist Project?	Teachers and other educators participating in the professional development	Motivation survey	Beginning of the school year
FIDELITY OF IMPLEMENTATION STUDY	What is the fidelity of implementation to the session design features?	Literacy specialist	Session implementation feedback forms	Following each professional development session
		Field faculty	Observations of literacy specialist' sessions; interviews of literacy specialists	During and after literacy specialists' professional development sessions with teachers
CHANGE IN TEACHER KNOWLEDGE STUDY	What is the influence of the professional development on participants' knowledge?	Teachers and other educators participating in the professional development	Core Curriculum Concepts Survey Interviews of literacy specialists and teachers	Beginning and end of the professional development After literacy specialists' professional development sessions with teachers; after field faculty's observation of teachers' field work implementation
CHANGE IN TEACHER PRACTICE STUDY	What is the influence of the professional development on teachers' practice?	Literacy specialists and teachers	Interviews of literacy specialists and teachers	After literacy specialists' professional development sessions with teachers; after field faculty's observation of teachers' field work implementation
			Teacher Learning Instrument [transcript analysis of lessons and postlesson conversations between literacy specialist and teachers]	Six-week period during the professional development sessions in the teaching domain

FIGURE 8.1. Research design for LS Project studies.

TABLE 8.1. Demographics of Literacy Specialists

	2000–2001 ($n = 125$)	2001–2002 ($n = 75$)	2002–2003 ($n = 153$)
Highest education degree			
Percent with master's	77	76	76
Percent with doctorate	—	3	2
Average years of teaching	19	20	19

ticipating literacy specialists, teachers, and other educators who were involved in the collaboration. As we expected, a greater number of literacy specialists held more advanced educational degrees and were more experienced than the teachers in their groups. The demographic profile of participants during the first 3 years showed that 76% of the literacy specialists held master's degrees and had been teaching an average of 19 years, compared to 47% of the teachers who held master's degrees and roughly 60% of the teachers who had less than 15 years of teaching experience.

For our purpose here, we describe the four studies that stem from our research questions, report the findings, and offer our interpretations. We also invite our readers to draw their own inferences, to question, and to critique our findings.

Teacher Motivation Study

In our investigation of what motivates teachers and other school-based educators to voluntarily participate in the LS Project, we used a 14-item survey that asked participants to rate factors on a Likert scale from 1 = little influence to 5 = great influence. We constructed the items for the survey based on commonly

TABLE 8.2. Demographics of Teachers

	2000–2001 ($n = 778$)	2001–2002 ($n = 631$)	2002–2004 ($n = 650$)
Highest education degree			
Percent with master's	42	48	52
Percent with doctorate	< 1	< 1	< 1
Years of Teaching			
Percent with 0–5 years	2	26	29
Percent with 6–15 years	67	35	32
Percent with 16–25 years	28	23	26
Percent with 26+ years	3	16	13

held intrinsic and external motivators of professional learning. We also included items that closely matched the incentives for participation that we communicated through presentations and brochures on the project. (See Chapter 7 for a discussion of the Motivation Survey.)

Using our network system, we administered the survey at the beginning of each year to all participants. In our October meeting with field faculty, we walked through the materials and procedures for administering the surveys. The field faculty, in turn, did the same at their meetings with the literacy specialists, who then followed suit at their next session with the teachers. We provided self-addressed stamped envelopes to facilitate the literacy specialists' prompt return of the completed surveys to the project office.

Findings

The most salient finding was that intrinsic motivators, those related to wanting to learn more and improve practice, were rated the highest by the participants. This finding was consistent over the 3 years, although the specific type of intrinsic motivators varied somewhat. Participants rated *improving teaching* and *learning new things* as the top two motivators over the 3 years. The third highest rated motivator in year 1 was *opportunities for discussion with colleagues*; in years 2 and 3, it was *opportunity for support from a literacy specialist*. The three lowest rated motivators were extrinsic. Over the 3 years these were consistently *administrator encouragement*, *peer encouragement*, and *financial reward*.

Implications

These findings are encouraging and support the idea that teachers, given the choice to participate in professional development, are intrinsically motivated to grow as professionals and want to do so through collaboration with their colleagues. Although reimbursement for participation in the professional development beyond the school day did occur in many districts, it is noteworthy that financial reward was not a major motivator for participation, nor was external press from administrators and colleagues. These findings underscore the need for professional development designers and implementers to assure that the participants' expectations for learning and collaboration will be met. Careful planning and embedding of relevant and meaningful learning activities are needed if the participants' motivation is to be sustained. To gauge how well participants' expectations are met throughout the professional development, planners and implementers need to monitor the implementation and use the feedback to make relevant adjustments. (Refer back to Chapter 7 for a description of the professional development monitoring system in the LS Project.)

Fidelity of Implementation Study

We learned from the motivation study that the participants were involved because they desired to learn more and to make improvements in their teaching. Sustaining their motivation depended largely on how well the sessions would be implemented according to the research-based design elements we integrated into the session learning activities and materials.

In our study of the extent to which the professional development was implemented according to its design, we used the literacy specialists' session implementation feedback forms (described in Chapter 7) and field faculty observations of literacy specialist–teacher sessions.

After each session the literacy specialists facilitated, they marked one of the following to indicate if they *Implemented as Designed*, *Modified*, or *Omitted* the main structural segments of a session: *Background*, *Goals*, *Vocabulary*, *Before*, *During*, *After*, *Reflection*, *Field Work*, and the materials provided with each session: activity sheets, transparencies, and videos. Spaces for comments on the feedback form prompted literacy specialists to explain when they omitted or modified any of the components and their reasons for doing so.

We analyzed a random sample of four sessions, one in each domain of the core curriculum (Sessions 1, 8, 10, and 13) and determined the percentage of *Implemented as Designed*, *Modified*, or *Omitted*. We also conducted a content analysis of the literacy specialists' comments to identify salient reasons for their omissions and modifications to the session components.

We learned more about the literacy specialists' session implementation and how they made instructional decisions through an analysis of the field faculty members' observations and interviews of literacy specialists. In addition to their monthly all-day meetings with the literacy specialists, we asked field faculty to conduct at least one observation of a literacy specialist facilitating a session in the teaching and assessing domains of the core curriculum, observe a teacher implementing the *Field Work* from that session, and follow up the observations with an interview of the literacy specialist and of the teacher. Our analyses of these data are limited to 12 literacy specialist and eight teacher observations and interviews across six of the 10 groups throughout the state.

Findings

For all 3 years, as shown in Table 8.3, the percentages for total implementation (including implemented as designed or modified) were greater than 84% for all structural segments. Implementation of the segments as designed was greater than 60%. Omitting basic components was consistently low, less than 14%. These percentages show a relatively strong level of implementation with a moderate degree of local adaptation of the components across the sessions over 3 years.

TABLE 8.3. Fidelity of Implementation

	2000–2001 (n = 106)	2001–2002 (n = 51)	2002–2003 (n = 72)
Session 1			
Implemented as designed	70	80	84
Modified	14	13	12
Session 8			
Implemented as designed	68	86	86
Modified	21	8	5
Session 10			
Implemented as designed	68	79	80
Modified	19	12	15
Session 13			
Implemented as designed	76	87	87
Modified	19	10	11

Note. Values represent percentage for type of implementation.

Our analysis of the literacy specialists' comments on the implementation feedback forms shed more light on the fidelity question. The types of modifications that literacy specialists' made included:

- Substituting one activity for another (e.g., examining writing samples from teachers' own classrooms rather than the ones provided in the session materials).
- Partially completing an activity due to time constraints.
- Reordering activities (e.g., integrating vocabulary during discussion throughout the session rather than at the beginning of the session).
- Extending an activity (e.g., using a website to feature more examples of parent resources).
- Adding an activity (e.g., including a matching vocabulary activity in addition to the K–W–L that was described in the session).
- Changing the format (e.g., conducting the activity in a whole group rather than in small groups).

When literacy specialists omitted components or activities, the major reason they did so was that they ran out of time.

Our analysis of the literacy specialists' interviews showed strong support for the quantitative findings on fidelity of implementation. Further, the analysis illuminated how they used the session materials and activities and which ones they considered important to the teachers. In the following two excerpts from interviews of literacy specialists, we glean insights into how they planned a session with their teachers in mind.

> I went through and I just kind of thought about how I would integrate those things [materials] into my group session. I read the literacy specialist notes [tips for implementation that supplemented the session materials], and I just kind of gleaned from those just what information was important to me. The types of things that I thought were going to be really, really relevant for the members of our group and the things that I thought were going to make a significant difference in the way that the teachers are teaching.

> I had worked with a group of teachers a couple of years ago on an After School Tutoring Program and we had assessment materials that I thought they had some good kind of definition type of things, and some illustrated things to use, so I used some of those materials rather than the wallet materials [articles included with the session materials].

The literacy specialists also commented on the articles, which they noted were an important resource for building background knowledge on the topic.

> I decide if I'm going to use that [the articles] for my own information, and I often use them as a really good discussion point and they've been helpful as background for me and then if it's not a lengthy article that's going to take a few trees to conquer then I share with them or if I think it's something they will probably read and sometimes I assigned readings in addition to *Field Work* if I really felt it was something important that they have to read and then we will discuss it.

> For the next session, I will give those articles to them [the teachers] ahead of time so we have a bigger time frame here to work with between now and the next lesson. So I will give them the articles from the wallet [the envelope that contained the session readings] so they can do some background reading.

Our analysis of the literacy specialists' interviews also illuminated the structural segments (*Before, During, After*) and learning activities that they thought were important to teachers' understanding.

> I will keep the *Before, During,* and *After*. I really believe in that type of framework. I think it's important they practice, maybe go through the activity themselves to understand it, and understand, put themselves in the place of how their students might feel in an activity.

> It is a short video [in the session], but it is important for them [the teachers] to see. And then we will talk about implications for us as teachers, and, then

summarize it and pull it all together, and what does this mean for us. And the reflection piece, I think that is *huge*, because unless we reflect on what we are doing and unless we reflect on what we just learned we never apply it.

In most instances, when the literacy specialists modified the session structure or its materials, they reportedly did so based on their own levels of familiarity with the content and their perceptions of what would work best with their respective teacher groups. The teachers, like the literacy specialists, commented on the learning activities that they found important to their understanding about literacy teaching and learning.

Well, I think the field assignments really required me to kind of stretch and not get too comfortable in doing things you know the same way you always do. It required you to do more you know different strategies and this whole idea of the protocol.

Studying the protocols [Sessions 9–12] helped me become aware of what I was doing, it really has. In looking at my [tran]scripts, I noticed things about my teaching. Stepping back and letting them [the students] do more. I think maybe that's my special education background. I don't give them more independence, let them make mistakes as much as I should, let them use strategies themselves and not just be in there so much.

Implications

Fidelity of implementation is an especially important consideration when widely disseminating a professional development model across multiple sites, as we are doing in the LS Project. The results we observed in the first 3 years of implementation are strong. They suggest that the network system seemed to be working. Field faculty members were disseminating the sessions to literacy specialists, who, in turn, were implementing them with relatively close adherence to the intended design. From the literacy specialists' interviews and comments about the professional development sessions, we can also see that they did not take a prescriptive approach in their implementation. They allowed for local input and responded to their participants' needs and interests. On the other hand, had we observed too little fidelity to the design, such a lack of consistency in the implementation would make it very difficult to support, monitor, and evaluate the implementation.

Change in Teacher Knowledge Study

To examine the influence of teachers' participation in the professional development on their learning, we developed a 24-item survey of key concepts taught in the core curriculum. (Refer back to Chapter 7.) We also analyzed the literacy specialist and teacher interview data gathered by the field faculty.

Findings

We compared the beginning- and end-of-year Concepts Survey scores using a paired samples *t*-test. The results of these analyses are shown in Table 8.4. In each year of the 3-year study, the results showed statistically significant positive differences between teachers' ratings of their conceptual understanding at the beginning and at the end of the professional development sessions.

To test for differences between the field faculty–literacy specialist–teacher groups, we conducted analysis of variance (ANOVA) and found no statistically significant differences between groups in years 1 or 2, but we did find significant differences between the groups in year 3, $F(9, 393) = 2.248; p = .019$). Further analysis showed that one group made lower gains compared to the others, although the difference between beginning and end concept scores within that group were statistically significant.

Results of the qualitative analyses indicated that teachers became more focused on student performance and learned new strategies. The major themes captured the teachers' comments on what they learned form their participation in the sessions. These themes were teaching as it relates to students' learning, refinements of current practices, and learning new strategies.

> [The professional development sessions] made me a better teacher. Gave me new information on how to teach in general. Helped me focus on where kids are and set individual goals. Gave me scaffolding and modeled instruction. I

TABLE 8.4. Concepts Survey Paired Samples *t*-Test

	Pre Total	Post Total	*t*-test Results
	Mean SD	Mean SD	*t* value
2000–2001 (*n* = 161)	56.72 12.05	52.66 11.64	8.635***
2001–2002 (*n* = 229)	56.76 13.76	49.66 11.61	9.265***
2002–2003 (*n* = 393)	63.20 13.89	47.77 11.33	23.17***

Note. Based on the rating scale, lower ratings indicate higher levels of conceptual understanding.
***$p < .001$.

was a Special Ed[ucation] teacher and thought all regular ed[ucation] kids were on the same level. They're not.

I've been learning more ways to teach them to attack, you know, word attack skills for this level child . . . strategies. We learned about stations and all that, which I still have to work out. I'm still old-fashioned that way. They do the computers later in the morning once they have finished their other work, they do go to the computers. It helped me with the reading . . . how to set up the reading books and how the children should pick and choose.

In their interviews the literacy specialists talked about the teachers gaining a better understanding of the literacy teaching concepts and how they applied them to their practice.

And we're finding, and you do it with your kids, we want your kids, students to use a larger word, then you start using that word and it just becomes ingrained within them. So, the more we use it [literacy terms used in the sessions], the more it will edge in to our professional talk. I think they responded in saying that they're starting to understand. At first, on Session 9, they were completely overwhelmed . . . as I was . . . of what protocols and scaffolding were. Then it became a little clearer in Session 10. And I believe now they are starting to feel like they are "getting it," and they're understanding this, and they're starting to put it to use. I think that we're making progress, and they're starting to say, now they are understanding.

Learning from the professional development was not only a matter of learning for teachers but also for the literacy specialists. Through their teaching of the sessions centered on the core curriculum, the literacy specialists were developing self-efficacy in their role of instructional leaders. For example:

The professional development confirms what I have been trying to accomplish this year, and what I have done in the past several years. It makes me stronger in my background information because I'm presenting it to others. I feel a real responsibility to get it right, because these people are asking me questions. I need to be sure of terms and information that I'm presenting. As far as collegial, it's really tied the four of us together. We have common background knowledge and we can share and really know what each other's thinking about certain parts of literacy. I think they [the teachers] enjoyed it. Every time they leave they tell me there's something new they're trying or thinking about differently; and I like to hear that. That they are thinking about approaching a lesson differently; and there is so much that we can't do it all at once, but even the little changes that they are more aware of, some of them have started audiotaping and listening. I don't know that they are to the point where they are actually going to transcribe, but they are making comments like,

"It's funny that I wanted to do this and it went this way," just reflecting on what they're doing. So they keep coming back and they keep asking to do more and they're planning for next year. So every time I leave I get the sense that it's making a difference, and it's changing how they're approaching their classroom thought process.

Implications

Given that change in teachers' knowledge is one of the outcomes of the professional development, it was essential that we try to measure how well it was achieved. The survey we developed on the concepts taught in the curriculum was one way to do this. The results were favorable, as indicated by the comparison of the beginning and end survey. Through the interviews of literacy specialists and teachers, we were able to learn more about the qualitative aspects of the yearlong program that engaged them in professional discourse and collaborative problem solving toward the shared goal of increasing knowledge about teaching reading and writing. These kinds of tools and methods for assessing outcomes in professional development are important to develop along with the content and the activities of the curriculum.

Change in Teacher Practice Study

As observed in the previous study, we have some evidence from interview and survey data that the professional development contributed to teachers' knowledge about literacy content and pedagogy. We observed in the interview data, too, that the professional development assisted the teachers in making instructional improvement.

For a more in-depth investigation of the question *What influence does the participation have on teacher practice?*, we turn to several studies that were conducted using the Teacher Learning Instrument (TLI; Rosemary et al., 2002). In Chapter 6, we described and illustrated the TLI in our example of Linda coaching Sharon in the *Field Work* for Comprehension, Session 11 in the professional development. The *Field Work* procedures in the teaching domain set up the conditions for the TLI, an inquiry process for closely examining teaching with the explicit goal of improving teaching to improve student learning. This structured inquiry process has four phases:

- Phase 1: The literacy specialist and teacher coplan a lesson, which includes identifying a specific teaching strategy and the scaffolding actions that the teacher intends to implement.
- Phase 2: The teacher teaches the lesson.

- Phase 3: The literacy specialist and the teacher independently analyze the lesson.
- Phase 4: The literacy specialist and the teacher engage in a debriefing conversation to further analyze, interpret, and evaluate the lesson.

The studies that were conducted on the use of TLI involved 12 participants, six pairs of literacy specialists and teachers who volunteered to engage in the TLI process over three consecutive lessons. The lesson transcripts juxtaposed with the debriefing conversation transcripts were the major sources of data in these studies.

Findings

We summarize the most useful findings from these studies to illustrate how the professional development set up a context of assisted performance as defined by Tharp and Gallimore (1988), in which literacy specialists and teachers intentionally came together around a shared goal: to improve teaching to improve student performance. The major findings include:

- *Focused conversations centered on artifacts of teaching and learning.* The lesson transcript served as an object of inquiry. It gave the teacher and the literacy specialist something specific and tangible to discuss. It set the lesson apart from the personal and allowed them to engage in an objective analysis of what had occurred in the lesson. Their conversations consistently focused on four topics: instructional goals (e.g., to improve students' fluency), analytical processes (e.g., how to discern patterns in teacher–student talk to improve teaching performance), appropriateness of materials (e.g., text difficulty), and student performance (e.g., how well the students accomplished the task).
- *Heightened awareness of teaching strategies.* The teachers became more attuned to features of effective instructional strategies and better able to identify when they did or did not use them in their own teaching. For example, over three lessons, the teachers became more adept at recognizing and naming teaching actions, such as focusing students' attention on the task, providing for sufficient practice, and monitoring independent performance.
- *Heightened awareness of scaffolding.* As teachers developed more skill in analyzing their lesson transcripts, later conversations with the literacy specialist were more focused than earlier ones on specific ways to scaffold student learning based on what they observed in their teaching. For example, the teachers became attuned to the amount of their talk compared to that of the students and the amount of wait time they allowed for students' responses. After they under-

stood how to discern evidence of scaffolding in their own lessons, they were better able to interpret the patterns and plan how to translate them to changes in practice.

- *Improved teaching skill.* The analysis of the lesson transcripts was a way to closely examine teaching, one turn-taking exchange at a time. This "poring over" the transcripts exposed the teacher–student and the student–student interactions. Such slowing down of teaching provoked changes in the teacher's actions. The mind-set on more specific teaching moves resulted in a more precise execution of a teaching strategy that led to improvements in students' performance, as observed in later lessons compared to earlier ones. The heightened awareness of scaffolding also led to improved performance. The teachers developed a better understanding of the ZPD as it relates to instructional level in the teaching of reading. For example, later lessons reflected changes in reading material to better support students' fluency development. There was also a shift in the types of praise, from general comments like "good job" to more specific attention to the students' developing skill.

Implications

The findings from the TLI studies are important in that they show the potential of inquiry tools to focus teachers' thinking about themselves as mediators of student learning and to make intentional adjustments in teaching that will lead to improved student performance. The analytical processes embedded in the TLI enhanced teachers' ability to self-regulate their teaching actions as a result of their structured conversations with the literacy specialists.

The research on effective professional development shows the potential of inquiry-based learning. In the LS Project we designed problem-solving activities to be conducted during the sessions as well as after the session through *Field Work* activities. How well the inquiry tools and strategies "do their job" depends on many factors, including the viability of the tools themselves, the know-how and skill of the professional developer to engage participants, the willingness of the participants to engage in the processes, and whether or not the participants adopt an inquiry approach to their own practice. These are questions we need to continue to address in our professional development project that aims to make a difference in teacher learning and practice.

Our analysis of the LS Project thus far is an initial step in demonstrating the efficacy of the statewide professional development initiative. We have made some progress on this agenda, but we still have a distance to go in examining the various components of the project and how they work together to create and sustain an effective professional development model. We discuss future research directions in the next section.

RESEARCH WE NEED

Teachers' professional development and learning have moved to center stage as key factors in promoting effective reading instruction. It is this interplay between the developing professional self and the challenge of new ideas that serves as the catalyst of change. An evidence-based understanding about how to help teachers develop and grow toward more expert forms of practice, however, is quite limited. This is understandable since teacher professional development as an object of study is a relatively recent phenomenon, only introduced into the teaching field toward the end of the 20th century (Randi & Zeichner, 2004; Sykes, 1996).

As summarized in the previous section, the research studies embedded in the LS Project strive to contribute to the research we have about teachers' motivations for embracing professional learning, about their knowledge gains through participation in professional development, and about the impact of certain professional development activities (e.g., coaching) on teachers' practices. At the same time, these inquiries point to the research we need if professional development programs are to make a difference in the instructional quality of classrooms and the professional lives of teachers. A few investigative areas have emerged for us as potential sites of future research that could expand an evidence-based understanding of professional growth and learning in reading pedagogy. Here are three that we think are especially needed.

Teacher Content Knowledge

We need to know more about the knowledge gains teachers make as a result of their participation in professional development programs. The essential question is: Do teachers acquire new teaching content knowledge through professional development?

The assumption is often made that the presentation of new information, new techniques, and new strategies leads effortlessly to new pedagogical knowledge constructions by teachers. Certainly, teachers know more about "what to do" after they experience professional development than they did before. Unfortunately, we have little real proof that this happens. Teachers may participate, but we do not know if their experience impacts what is referred to as *pedagogical content knowledge*, or *how to* represent and formulate subject matter in ways that make it comprehensible to others and *to better* understand what makes the learning of specific topics easy or difficult for learners (Shulman, 1986, 1987).

One of the stumbling blocks in examining the relationships between professional development activity and its impact on teacher content knowledge is instrumentation (Phelps & Schilling, 2004). Measures for assessing teacher content knowledge prior to, during, and following professional development programs in general are lacking, and those that can accomplish this task accurately, sensitively, and adequately are rare. The field needs better measures—and more investigative effort needs to be applied to the design and testing of reliable, valid assessments of teachers' content knowledge gains in the professional development context. Some steps have been made in this direction, such as assessing teachers' specialized linguistic knowledge (Fillmore & Snow, 2000), but more attention must be directed to what teachers know about the *content* of reading and how this knowledge is used in practice.

Forms of Assistance

We need to know more about how to assist teachers toward achieving more expert performance, and what a developmental *continuum of assisted performance* might look like. Faced with the challenges of the No Child Left Behind Act, many states and school districts have identified the literacy coach role as a viable means of delivering high-powered professional development in classroom reading instruction to meet the demands of science-based reading instruction. Some research (e.g., Joyce & Showers, 1995) illustrates the benefits of coaching for helping teachers transfer new knowledge and skills to everyday practice. Yet specifics about the literacy coach role in schools are not well documented. Criteria for preparing literacy coaches have only recently become available (Bean, 2004; International Reading Association, 2004b), and research-based information on effective coaching models is formative at best. Given the growing investment in literacy coaches, particularly in beginning reading instruction, it is critical to examine the characteristics of the role and the conditions that support or constrain it in schools. We need to know much more about (1) coach responsibilities, key activities, how time is spent, and how teachers are coached; (2) the powerful setting influences that can support or constrain literacy coaches, thus impacting their efficacy; and (3) the critical domains of advanced professional education that prepare literacy coaches for their leadership role.

We also need to examine less intensive forms of assistance that also may suffice—for example, grade-level meetings, peer-led study groups, eLearning opportunities, electronic professional development tutorials on specific topics (e.g., reciprocal teaching), and material resources (e.g., checklists). Evidence that these less-elaborate forms of assistance support teachers' use of more efficacious instructional techniques and strategies is growing. The venue of eLearning, for example, shows increasing promise for stimulating teachers' intentions to apply research-based techniques to their practice (Lenhart et al., 2005). Similarly, development of audio lesson analysis skills appears to improve coaches' abilities to identify teaching actions that promote students' learning

(Rosemary, 2005). Other studies indicate the utility of checklists as feedback mechanisms for self-regulation and self-assessment (e.g., Au & Carroll, 1997).

What we know about these forms of learning support (e.g., their design and power), however, is quite scant, and more evidence is needed, not only about the potentialities of different forms of assistance but also about how these might be organized to represent a continuum of assisted performance for teacher development and change.

Disposition to Learn from Experience

We need to know more about how to cultivate the teachers' dispositions for critical thinking and reflection so they might learn from their own experience. Too often in meeting the demands for teachers to know more (and still more) and to grow more skillful as reading teachers, this dimension of professional development and learning is overlooked. Yet it is essential if teachers' growing knowledge and skill (their abilities) are to be judiciously applied in everyday instruction. For this, teachers need to develop a critical stance in order to use sound judgment at those inevitable crucial decision points in instruction. (Should I press on, or fall back and let new ideas gel? Should I explain or allow discovery at this point? Should more time be allotted for practice or is this enough?) In the end, there is no "script" for effective teaching, only plans for composing what will become today's lesson via the exercise of judgment.

How to design professional learning for teachers so as to instill a critical stance toward one's own learning and experience, and therefore developing judging abilities, is a difficult professional development problem, and one that is understudied. We have some general information about how to do this. Teachers need *time*, for example, to internalize new concepts and represent them in their own practice. They need opportunities to *reflect*, accompanied by feedback that scaffolds reflection from the technical and perfunctory to consideration of standards and ethical criteria. They need to participate in demonstrations of *critical thinking* about instructional problems and procedures (think-alouds) that make visible the judgment-making processes to be exercised in classroom contexts (Ball & Cohen, 1999; Sykes, 1999).

But we do not know enough about the details of these process elements to deliberately and systematically use them in cultivating teachers' dispositions toward critique over blind acceptance of prevailing approaches; toward adaptation over strict adherence to procedures; toward generating new knowledge over rigid implementation of knowledge given. In designing professional development approaches and programs, it is not clear (at all) about how to foster a *pedagogical critical awareness* that nurtures habits of asking and debating, a discourse of conjecture and deliberation, a stance of critique and inquiry. We need research that helps us to understand the patterns of interaction in schools that foster a critical stance. We need research that examines discourse shifts in teachers' problem solving, analyses of student work, and reflection statements in professional learning contexts, such as grade-level meetings or coaching sessions, that sheds light on how professional development helps teachers learn from their own experience. And we need research that better specifies how to design professional development in ways that remain open to new ideas and insights, to new images of implementation and practice, and the role of judgment in instructional decision making.

CLOSING

Donald Schon (1987) argued that in a science of teaching we also need artistry. To apply scientifically based reading research in everyday reading instruction requires the art of identifying the instructional problems confronting us, such as issues of diversity, poverty, shrinking resources, and social complexities. It requires the art of implementation that judiciously applies evidence-based techniques and strategies to bring all learners forward. And it requires the art of improvisation where individual teachers use their creativity, their imagination, and their experience to create optimal conditions so that students learn to read and write, not only to achieve, but also to enjoy what literacy has to offer.

In the LS Project we seek to understand both the science and the art of effective primary-grade instruction and to provide professional development and learning that helps teachers grow in each of these dimensions of practice. To this purpose we pursue a research agenda that informs our professional work, contributes to a growing body of knowledge on professional development models, provides evidence for effective program design, and reveals research we need.

Going Live with Martin
Inside Session 9, Teaching Oral Language

To "watch" this session, we will follow a fictitious professional developer, Martin, the school reading tutor. He was asked by the principal to lead this professional development effort and has already presented the introduction and the first eight sessions of the knowing and planning domains to the 10 K–3 teachers in his school. The teachers had participated in a schoolwide teacher learning group the previous year but were anxious to continue professional development designed for early elementary teachers. They have met in their classrooms every other week since the beginning of school. The classroom teachers alternate sharing how the new learning experiences are influencing their classroom instruction.

Martin reviewed the curriculum materials and has planned the session presentations to meet the needs of his learners who have expressed an interest in improving their teaching skills. He has noticed that the teachers use a variety of flashy instructional strategies that seem to interest the children but are not necessarily producing strong readers and writers. He has been looking forward to the teaching domain because it focuses on both the content of literacy and effective teaching skills.

SESSION BACKGROUND

Prior to presenting this session, Martin studied the curriculum *Background Information* on acknowledging curriculum expectations and reviewed all materials listed on the *Bookshelf*. Based on his knowledge of the teacher learners, he then planned the session and gathered the materials listed in the session folder. Having just completed the planning domain, the teachers have critically reviewed their classroom materials and organization, and they have thought about how standards guide instruction and student's home environments influence learning.

BEFORE SESSION ACTIVITIES:
SHARE–INTRODUCE–EXPLAIN/SHOW

Martin began the session with a discussion of the findings from the previous *Field Work* assignment for which participants were asked to design an activity that would be appropriate for home use. He asked the teachers to evaluate what they had learned thus far and how it represents the knowledge base for planning literacy education. They discussed the importance of striving to provide excellent literacy education for all children and about the consequences of not grounding instructional planning in the knowledge base.

It was Mrs. Johnson's turn to demonstrate how the professional development has increased learning in her classroom. She showed teachers a classroom newsletter sent to student's families and explained how it seems to have increased student enthusiasm for reading at home. Children are reading both independently and with an adult more than her previous record keeping indicated.

Martin then introduced the session topic, Teaching Oral Language. He reviewed the *Professional Learning Goals* of the session and pointed out how the *Before, During,* and *After* session activities will help them achieve the learning goals. As they had done in previous sessions, the teachers stopped to write new session vocabulary words in a word journal. Martin offers peppermint candies as a reward to teachers when he hears them use new vocabulary words in discussions. He then read the children's picture book *Elbert's Bad Word* by Audrey Wood, reminding teachers to never underestimate the power of words.

Martin went on to explain to the participants that the next four sessions would focus on the teaching of oral language, words, reading comprehension, and writing. He noted that a more in-depth look at assessment would be the focus of Sessions 13–15, building on the assess–plan–teach cycle of diagnostic teaching. He presented the overview of teaching literacy that involves the interaction between the goal, the content, and the instruction that takes place through the purposeful planning of and executing of teaching strategies. He also explained that the emphasis of the teaching sessions would be on what teachers *do* and *say* to guide and support children's learning. Goals were defined and the oral language, words, comprehension, and writing content were reviewed. Martin emphasized the need to identify learning expectations (English language arts standards, benchmarks, and indicators), the need to know the content of literacy instruction (what concepts and skills need to be taught), and the need to thoroughly understand the information and ideas contained in the subject matter they are teaching. He also explained how effective literacy instruction involves the careful implementation of teaching strategies that take place within the before–during–after lesson framework. He continued by introducing the idea of a lesson protocol as the basic organizational sequence for executing effective strategies and scaffolding as the instructional components that support student learning and discussing the interrelationships between protocol and scaffolding.

Teachers were then introduced to the literacy lesson protocol as the basic organizational sequence for the teaching strategies that are executed within the before–during–

after framework. Martin explained that "protocol" is a label for a set of teaching moves that are embedded in effective teaching strategies. Teachers were asked to provide everyday examples in which they use protocols in their teaching.

Martin described the concept of scaffolding as another critical element of literacy instruction because it refers to the deliberate supports teachers provide in pulling forward student learning. The terms were discussed. Scaffolding was explained as the process that takes place within the lesson framework, as the fuel that drives the lesson forward. He discussed the scaffolding components that provide assistance until the child can do the task independently. He noted that lessons should take place in the student's ZPD and that instruction must remain there in order to be effective. Martin emphasized the constructivist model script of *prompt–encourage–add to* in which teachers *prompt* children for their responses, *encourage* them to explain, and *add to* what children say so as to extend ideas and information. They discussed how the constructivist model differs from the transmission model (the recitation script of teacher–student exchanges typically found in the transmission model of teaching has a predictable, repeated initiation–response–evaluation [IRE] pattern: teacher *initiation* is followed by student *response*, which is followed by teacher *evaluation*).

Martin pointed out that we should find evidence of both protocol and scaffolding in the teacher and student interaction during a lesson. He emphasized how performance is assisted through the interactions, giving an example of how a student's performance is supported when a teacher gives feedback to a child's response. Teachers were asked to think about their own talk and the presence of scaffolding in their interactions with children, and then to provide examples.

Martin told teachers that the session on oral language begins with a review of the oral language development continuum discussed in Session 1. Teachers identified benchmarks in oral language development and discussed the adult's role in teaching children to talk and listen and the actions that seem to be at the heart of teaching children language. He gave an example of how the adult tends to provide a model, such as, "Say thank-you to Grandma," and encourage children to repeat and practice until they can use the appropriate language on their own. He highlighted the importance of providing a model, or script, for children to follow and ample practice so they learn how to say what they want and need to say effectively.

The session continued as the group examined the goal, content, and instruction of teaching oral language. Teachers reviewed the Communication: Oral and Visual Standard as the teaching goal and explored the content of oral language instruction by noting that different language functions emphasize different kinds of talk. Martin explained how the language of literacy often involves *describing, narrating, reporting, reciting*, and *presenting*; how the language of inquiry relies on *questioning, classifying, explaining, connecting*, and *comparing*; and how the language of social interaction includes *sharing, discussing, conversing, directing*, and *attending*. He continued by looking at oral language instruction, then by reviewing how effective teaching strategies are organized and implemented using lesson protocols and how student learning is assisted through scaffolding. He focused on the basic protocol of oral language instruction. Teachers were told that they will explore the protocol in relation to three broad oral language uses in the classroom: for literacy (developing reading and writing), for inquiry, and for social interaction. Martin pointed out that the protocol is common to these uses of language and supports children's speaking and listening skills for these purposes.

Martin presented three language protocols and examples of effective teaching strategies. He then reviewed each one and described how the protocols and scaffolding should guide instruction of listening and speaking. The group discussed what the teacher might say to encourage children's use of oral language in each of the functions and how teachers might assess a child's performance. They then talked about how the language of literacy protocol would guide the teaching of oral language and help students to meet expectations. Teachers added other strategies that could be used to develop oral language.

To further demonstrate what teachers say and do as they teach, Martin presented a transcript of classroom talk. Teachers were asked to role-play the transcript three times to draw attention to the children's language. He then used the following probes to help them describe it: Are children using language to tell a story? To solve a problem? To work together on a project? He underlined examples in the transcript to support the responses and identified the grade-level indicators (grades 3–4) being addressed. The primary language function was recorded at the top of the transcript. Martin demonstrated how to code the talk for evidence of a protocol by writing P1 next to statements in the transcript where the teacher *focused attention* and P2 when the teachers *explained* the language function. He explained to teachers that teacher–child exchanges or patterns of exchanges show how a teacher scaffolds learning. He used the scaffolding codes to mark the talk for evidence of scaffolding features, noting that the codes may not apply to all instances of the talk, and that more than one code may be applied to some instances of the talk. He emphasized that while a teacher may follow an instructional protocol, it is the effective use of scaffolding that leads a child from assisted to independent performance. To find evidence of learning, they examined the child's performance as indicated in the transcript.

DURING SESSION ACTIVITIES: ORGANIZE–DO–RECORD

The teachers broke up into small groups to examine transcripts of two different oral language-based instructional events: a picture walk (literacy) and a group discussion (social). They role-played each sample transcript at least twice, then identified the grade-level indicators and the language function of each sample, paying close attention to the teacher's and the children's talk. Teachers coded one transcript for protocol and scaffolding components found in the teacher's talk and interactions with children. They also underlined the children's talk to assess the children's performance.

AFTER SESSION ACTIVITIES: PRESENT–DISCUSS–SUMMARIZE

The teachers reconvened as a large group to review each oral language sample. They identified the language function of each and pointed to examples in the teacher's and the children's talk. Coded excerpts of teacher instruction that occurred in the oral language activity were shared. They had a discussion about the importance of the teacher's role as a language model and as a conversational partner. Using the analysis of the transcript, teachers assessed how well the teacher encouraged the students' language and supported development. Martin encouraged the teachers to explain their analytical process and shared observations from the transcript to support their interpretations. The group discussion continued as teachers explored what would be needed to be more precise in teaching to develop student's oral language skills and how teachers may assess the children's oral language skills.

To conclude the session, Martin reviewed the oral language protocol and described language functions and related talk in the classroom setting. He asked the teachers to recall the procedure for locating protocol features and scaffolding features in a transcript of an instructional event. Martin then restated major points about oral language development and teaching in the lesson. Remaining questions were answered.

TO THE CLASSROOM

Teachers left the session with two assignments. The first assignment was to continue reflecting in the journals they started in Session 1. They were asked to summarize the key points, highlight new insights, note questions that emerged, and react on a personal level to the context, content, or strategies used in the session. The second assignment was to complete *Field Work* designed to extend learning to the classroom. Martin stated that the purpose of the *Field Work* was to analyze an excerpt of oral language teaching. He told teachers to design a standards-based oral language lesson that represents one of the three language functions: literacy, inquiry, or social interaction. They were asked to listen to an audiotape recording of the lesson and then to prepare a written transcript of 5–10 minutes of the lesson that represented ample teacher and child interaction. After marking the transcript using the protocol and scaffolding codes, the teachers were told to respond to the following questions: What components were present? How often? What components were not present? They were asked to add a brief reflection that discussed their interpretation of the lesson. Then they were asked to answer another set of questions: What did you observe about the child's use of language? How would you assess the child's use of language? How well does the child perform in relation to the expected level of performance? What changes do you need to make in the future? Why? Overall, how effective was your lesson?

In addition to assignments designed to support learning, Martin scheduled classroom visits during which he offered help to the teachers as they began to plan instruction based on standards. He spent one full day every week in each school in order to be available to model instruction, to help locate appropriate materials, and to answer questions. Checklists itemizing effective classroom instruction served as a guide for evaluation and conferences designed to probe self-evaluation encouraged reflection. (See Chapter 6.) Martin encouraged teachers to assess their ability to use new knowledge in the classroom setting and urged them to assess student learning that may result from effective teaching skills.

BEYOND THE CLASSROOM

Martin made every effort during and after the session to introduce teachers to multiple paths to professional development. He shared journal articles and professional videos demonstrating classroom literacy instruction. He also suggested that the teachers explore the challenge presented in the *Making Connections* task, which asked them to imagine that they were the chair of the K–3 reading curriculum committee and a controversy is swirling around the extent to which oral language instruction should be represented in the curriculum. They were to make the case for including oral language in the curriculum at the grade level they teach, with an eye to the English language arts standards, and to articulate the features of oral language teaching and learning that influence literacy achievement.

Martin also scheduled classroom visits to demonstrate use of protocol and scaffolding techniques. He then provided support for teachers as they examined their own teaching for evidence of student learning. Teachers excelled as the professional development created a learning environment in which they could assume responsibility for improving their teaching practice.

REFLECTION AND RECORD KEEPING

After the session, Martin checked attendance sheets and evaluated the session by reflecting on the quality of his presentation of materials and on the degree of participant learning that was evident throughout activities. He recorded his observations, thoughts, ideas, and interpretations of the session in his journal. To assess the presentation, he responded to the following questions: Did I feel comfortable with the concepts and content of the session? Was my presentation style and format appropriate for the group? Did my questions stimulate thinking? Were my directions clearly stated? What part of the presentation was outstanding? What part of the presentation could be improved?

To assess participant learning, he reviewed the *Professional Learning Goals* of the session to identify ways in which he could "see" the application of key concepts to participants' classroom instruction. As he visited classrooms during the following few weeks, he watched for evidence of instruction guided by children's developmental strengths and needs; he also noted evidence of teachers engaging in self-assessment of their own teaching.

Because Martin is participating in a larger scale professional development initiative, he also completed and submitted the required session feedback form for this session. His responses, which indicated his use and implementation of session materials, will be combined with other presenter responses to serve as an evaluation and research tool for the professional development curriculum planners.

APPENDIX B

Going Live with Stephanie
Inside Session 5,
Acknowledging Curriculum Expectations

To "watch" this session, we will follow a fictitious professional developer, Stephanie, the school district's literacy specialist. She was asked by the district's director of elementary curriculum to lead this professional development effort and has already presented the introduction and four sessions of the knowing domain to 40 teachers from the five elementary schools in the district. Participation is required for the teachers, so Stephanie presents the curriculum in 3-hour sessions to three different groups at three different locations. One group of 10 teachers from one school attends Saturday morning sessions twice a month. Another group of 15 meets every other Monday after school. The other 15 teachers from two different schools alternate meeting at one school the first Thursday of the month and at the other school on the third Thursday of the month.

After reviewing the curriculum materials, Stephanie chose to focus on the assess–plan–teach cycle throughout the sessions as it is most likely to be a new concept for most teachers. She planned the session presentations to meet the needs of her learners: they are faced with large classes and have few resources. Some participants have appeared to be comfortable working with peers in a professional development situation, other have been concerned about the amount of time they are spending. She decided to carefully review teacher reflections to look for ways to help teachers address these concerns.

SESSION BACKGROUND

Prior to presenting this session, Stephanie studied the curriculum *Background Information* on acknowledging curriculum expectations and reviewed all materials listed on the *Bookshelf*. Based on her knowledge of the teacher learners, she then planned the session and gathered materials listed in the session folder. Group leaders at each school sent out reminders a few days prior to the session.

BEFORE SESSION ACTIVITIES:
SHARE–INTRODUCE–EXPLAIN/SHOW

Stephanie began the session with a discussion of the findings from the previous *Field Work* assignment for which they were asked to evaluate models and methods found in their classroom reading program. The discussion continued as teachers explained how student learning expectations were described in the materials they examined and shared their thought on the standards movement.

Stephanie then introduced the session topic, Acknowledging Curriculum Expectations. She reviewed the *Professional Learning Goals* of the session, and then pointed out how the *Before*, *During*, and *After* session activities will help the teachers achieve their learning goals. To present the session *Vocabulary*, she asked individuals to complete a vocabulary word and definition match worksheet, and locate an example in *Ohio Academic Content Standards: K–12 English Language Arts*. She then read *Testing Miss Malarkey* by Judy Finchler. This humorous picture book, suggested in *Bright Starters*, highlights the commotion surrounding standardized testing. After pointing out that there are standards at the national, state, and district levels for both students and teachers, she briefly discussed the need to know these standards and to explore the dilemmas they pose for teachers. She continued the topic of standards by comparing sets of student learning expectations at the national level, at the state level, and at the district level. As the teachers examined the standards, Stephanie asked the following questions:

1. What goal does the standard set?
2. How worthy is the goal?
3. How can the goal be achieved?
4. How can it be assessed?
5. How does it align with the developmental continuum from Session 1?

Stephanie reminded the teachers that standards influence everyday practice. Then she emphasized the concept that what students need to know and be able to do implies what teachers need to know and be able to do in order to effectively pull children toward meeting learning expectations. She illustrated this connection by helping teachers complete the activity page "Core Curriculum Links between Ohio English Language Arts Standards: K–3 Benchmarks." Teachers were also asked to read the Phonemic Awareness, Word Recognition, and Fluency standards and benchmarks. Next, she commented on how teachers' knowledge and skills work in conjunction with standards to guide literacy instruction and described what teachers need to know about phonemic awareness, word recognition, and fluency. As a group, Stephanie and the teachers noted approaches to planning and teaching that would support development in these areas. Finally, they determined how to assess what a student knows about decoding and fluent reading. Together, they followed through by completing the links with the other standards. The explanation continued as they explored links between teachers' knowledge and skills by focusing on standards-based lesson planning. Stephanie briefly discussed the phases of the writing process, then read the standard, the benchmark, and the indicators on a sample lesson plan. She asked the teachers what they would expect to see as the focus of instruction in the lesson and previewed the remaining parts of the lesson plan. She continued by showing teachers a video clip of a second-grade writing lesson on editing that addresses the Writing Process Standard.

DURING SESSION ACTIVITIES: ORGANIZE–DO–RECORD

Following the video, the teachers broke into small groups of threes and fours to critique instruction observed in the video clip of the writing lesson. After they shared their observations of the video lesson, Stephanie showed the video again, pausing for the groups to discuss evidence of the indicator being addressed. After the video, the groups recorded the evidence and responded to the following questions on the activity sheet:

What were the specific teaching actions you observed?

What were the children saying and doing?

What was the evidence of scaffolding?

What stage of word knowledge/orthographic development would be needed for children to apply this strategy successfully?

How will you help a child narrow his or her search to only a few words if there are many misspellings?

What other word-solving strategies might the child use to "get to" the correct spelling of a word?

How will you scaffold individual children as they apply this strategy during writer's workshop?

AFTER SESSION ACTIVITIES: PRESENT–DISCUSS–SUMMARIZE

Groups were then given an opportunity to present activity results to the whole group. Stephanie asked each group to present its findings and to build on the previous group's presentation as they shared their responses to the writing video lesson in their small-group activity.

The presentations led into a discussion that emphasized the key features of national, state, and local standards. Stephanie related these back to the teachers' earlier ideas about how learning expectations, curriculum, instruction, and assessment need to be aligned. She noted any new information and insights and discussed the questions that teachers had asked earlier in the session, and she tried to answer them. The teachers viewed the video again to look for ways to document evidence of student learning and ways to chart progress over time. She asked them to reflect on what the teacher needs to know to carry out the lesson effectively and ways to self-critique the effectiveness of the strategies.

To conclude the session, Stephanie reviewed the purpose of learning expectations (standards) and their role in literacy teaching. She recalled observations from experience and from the small-group activity, highlighting key features and themes. Remaining questions about standards were resolved.

TO THE CLASSROOM

Teachers left the session with two assignments. The first assignment was to continue reflecting on the session in the journals they started in Session 1. They were asked to summarize the key points, highlight new insights, note questions that emerged, and react on a personal level to the context, content, or strategies used in the session. The second assignment was to complete *Field Work* designed to extend learning to the classroom. Stephanie stated that the purpose of the *Field Work* was to plan and conduct a standards-based lesson. She told the teachers to select an English language arts standard and use its benchmarks and grade-level indicators to guide a lesson plan. To complete the plan, they were to specify the focus of instruction, describe the lesson, list the required materials, indicate the before–during–after lesson procedures, define how students will be observed and assessed, and describe self-critiquing methods. Using the plan, they were instructed to conduct the lesson and reflect on the lesson in relation to student performance and effectiveness in their own teaching. A *Field Work* assignment recording sheet was provided and teachers were asked to be prepared to discuss their results at the next session.

In addition to assignments designed to support learning, Stephanie scheduled classroom visits during which she offered help as teachers began to plan instruction based on standards. She spent time every week in each school in order to be available to the teachers to model instruction, to help locate appropriate materials, and to answer their questions. Checklists itemizing effective classroom instruction served as a guide for evaluation, and conferences designed to probe self-evaluation encouraged reflection. Stephanie encouraged teachers to assess their ability to use new knowledge in the classroom setting and also encouraged them to assess student learning that may result from effective teaching skills.

BEYOND THE CLASSROOM

Stephanie made every effort during and after the session to introduce teachers to multiple paths to professional development. She copied journal articles related to standards-based instruction to share with the teachers and led them to important websites addressing standards.

She suggested that the teachers explore the challenge presented in the *Making Connections* task, which asked them to prepare a 5-minute presentation that convinces their district's board of education that the standards are embedded in their everyday teaching work by providing the board with information on how teachers use the standards for planning language arts instruction and making sure that their students are achieving progress toward the benchmarks. Stephanie also led a monthly teacher learning group to guide teachers in the exploration of technology including eLearning. She hoped to create a learning environment in which teachers will eventually assume full responsibility for their professional development and are encouraged to take on leadership roles of their own.

REFLECTION AND RECORD KEEPING

After the session, Stephanie checked attendance sheets and evaluated the session by reflecting on the quality of her presentation of materials and on the degree of participant learning that was evident throughout the activities. She recorded her observations, thoughts, ideas, and interpretations of the session in her journal. To assess the presentation, she responded to the following questions: Did I feel comfortable with the concepts and content of the session? Was my presentation style and format appropriate for the group? Did my questions stimulate thinking? Were my directions clearly stated? What part of the presentation was outstanding? What part of the presentation could be improved?

To assess participant learning, she reviewed the professional learning goals of the session to identify ways in which she could "see" the application of key concepts to participants' classroom instruction. As she visited classrooms during the following few weeks, she watched for evidence of teacher instruction guided by children's strengths and needs; she also noted evidence of teachers engaging in self-assessment of their own teaching.

Because Stephanie is participating in a larger scale professional development initiative, she also completed and submitted the required session feedback form for this session. Her responses, which indicated her use and implementation of session materials, will be combined with other literacy specialist responses to serve as an evaluation and research tool for the professional development curriculum planners.

References

Abelmann, C., & Elmore, R. (1999). *When accountability knocks, will anyone answer?* (CPRE Research Report Series RR-42). Philadelphia: University of Pennsylvania, Graduate School of Education Consortium for Policy Research in Education.

Adams, M. J. (1990). *Beginning to read: Thinking and learning about print.* Cambridge, MA: MIT Press.

American Federation of Teachers. (1995). *Principles for professional development.* Washington, DC: Author.

Anderson, L. W., & Krathwohl, D. R. (Eds.). (2001). *A taxonomy for learning, teaching, and assessing: A revision of Bloom's Taxonomy of Educational Objectives* (complete ed.). New York: Longman.

Applebee, A. N. (1996). *Curriculum as conversation: Transforming traditions of teaching and learning.* Chicago: University of Chicago Press.

Au, K., & Carroll, J. (1997). Improving literacy achievement through a constructivist approach: The KEEP Demonstration Classroom Project. *Elementary School Journal, 97,* 205–221.

Ball, D. L., & Cohen, D. (1999). Developing practice, developing practitioners: Toward a practice-based theory of professional education. In L. Darling-Hammond & G. Sykes (Eds.), *Teaching as the learning profession: Handbook of policy and practice* (pp. 3–32). San Francisco: Jossey-Bass.

Bean, R. (2004). *The reading specialist: Leadership for the classroom, school, and community.* New York: Guilford Press.

Bear, D. (2001). "Learning to fasten the seat of my union suit without looking around": The synchrony of literacy development. *Theory into Practice, 30,* 149–157.

Beck, I., McKeown, M., Hamilton, R., & Kucan, L. (1998, Spring–Summer). Getting at the meaning: How to help students unpack difficult text. *American Educator,* pp. 66–77.

Berk, L. E., & Winsler, A. (1995). *Scaffolding children's learning: Vygotsky and early childhood education.* Washington, DC: National Association for the Education of Young Children.

Block, C., Oakar, M., & Hurt, N. (2002). The expertise of literacy teachers: A continuum from preschool to grade 5. *Reading Research Quarterly, 37,* 178–206.

Bloom, B. (1999). *Wolf!* New York: Orchard Books.

Borko, H. (2004). Professional development and teacher learning: Mapping the terrain. *Educational Researcher, 33,* 3–15.

Bransford, J. D., Brown, A. L., & Cocking, R. R. (Eds.). (2000). *How people learn: Brain, mind, experience, and school.* Washington, DC: National Academy Press.

Bronfenbrenner, U. (1994). Ecological models of human development. In T. Husten & T. N. Posteltheaite (Eds.), *International encyclopedia of education* (2nd ed., pp. 3–27). Oxford, UK: Pergamon Press.

Bronfenbrenner, U. (1995). Developmental ecology through space and time: A future perspective. In P. Moen, G. H. Elder, K. Luscher, & U. Bronfenbrenner, *Examining lives in context: Perspectives on the ecology of human development* (pp. 619–647). Washington, DC: American Psychological Association.

Bronfenbrenner, U., & Morris, P. A. (1998). The ecology of developmental processes. In W. Damon & R. M. Lerner (Eds.), *Handbook of child psychology* (5th ed.): *Vol. 1. Theoretical models of human development* (pp. 993–1028). New York: Wiley.

Brookfield, S. (1986). *Understanding and facilitating adult learning.* San Francisco: Jossey-Bass.

Burden, P. R., & Byrd, D. M. (1990). *Methods for effective teaching* (2nd ed.). Boston: Allyn & Bacon.

Butler, A., & Turbill, J. (1984). The reading–writing process. In *Towards a reading–writing classroom* (pp. 11–20). Portsmouth, NH: Heinemann.

Button, K., Johnson, J., & Furgerson, P. (1999). *Interactive writing in a primary classroom.* In *Reading research anthology: The why? of reading instruction* (pp. 200–215). Novato, CA: Arena Press.

Calkins, L., & Harwayne, S. (1987). *The writing workshop: A World of difference. A guide for staff development.* Portsmouth, NH: Heinemann.

Capra, F. (1996). *The web of life* (pp. 37, 39). New York: Doubleday.

Clay, D. (2002, May). *Database decision-making for educators.* Presentation at the Literacy Specialist Conference, Columbus, OH.

Collins, J. (2001). *Good to great: Why some companies make the leap . . . and others don't.* New York: HarperCollins.

Corcoran, T. B., & Goertz, M. E. (1995). Instructional capacity and high performance schools. *Educational Researcher, 24,* 27–31.

Costa, A. L., & Kallick, B. (Eds.). (1995). *Assessment in the learning organization: Shifting the paradigm.* Alexandria, VA: Association for Supervision and Curriculum Development.

Crockett, M. D. (2002). Inquiry as professional development: Creating dilemmas through teachers' work. *Teaching and Teacher Education, 18,* 609–624.

Cronin, D. (2000). *Click, clack, moo.* New York: Simon & Schuster.

Danielson, C. (1996). *Enhancing professional practice: A framework for teaching.* Alexandria, VA: Association for Supervision and Curriculum Development.

Dewey, J. (1933). *How we think: A restatement of the relation of reflective thinking to the educative process.* Lexington, MA: D. C. Heath.

Dewey, J. (1964). *John Dewey on education: Selected writings* (p. 70). Edited and with an introduction by Reginald D. Archambault. New York: Modern Library.

Dickinson, D. K., & Neuman, S. B. (Eds.). (2005). *Handbook of early literacy research* (Vol. 2.). New York: Guilford Press.

Erikson, E. (1985). *The life cycle completed: A review.* New York: Norton.

Fernandez, C., Cannon, J., & Chokshi, S. (2003). A US–Japan lesson study collaboration reveals critical lenses for examining practice. *Teaching and Teacher Education, 19,* 171–185.

Fillmore, L. W., & Snow, C. E. (2000). *What teachers need to know about language.* Washington, DC: Center for Applied Linguistics.

Firestone, W. A., & Pennell, J. R. (1997). Designing state-sponsored teacher networks: A comparison of two cases. *American Educational Research Journal, 34,* 237–266.

Fishman, S. M., & McCarthy, L. P. (1998). *John Dewey and the challenge of classroom practice.* New York: Teachers College Press.

Galdone, P. (1986). *The elves and the shoemaker.* Boston: Clarion Books.

Gallimore, R. (2003, May). *Professional development and literacy.* Presentation at the Literacy Specialist Conference, Columbus, OH.

Gallimore, R., & Goldenberg, C. N. (2001). Analyzing cultural models and settings to connect minority achievement and school improvement research. *Educational Psychologist, 36,* 45–56.

Goldenberg, C. N. (2006, May). *Successful school change: Creating settings to improve teaching and learning.* Presentation at the Literacy Specialist Conference, Columbus, OH.

Goldenberg, C. N., & Gallimore, R. (1991). Changing teaching takes more than a one-shot workshop. *Educational Leadership, 49,* 69–72.

Hart, B. (2000). A natural history of early language experience. *Topics in Early Childhood Special Education, 20,* 28–32.

Hart, B., & Risley, T. (1995). *Meaningful differences in the everyday experience of young children.* Baltimore: Brookes.

Hawley, W. (2005, May) *Learner-centered professional development and continuous school improvement.* Presentation at the Literacy Specialist Conference, Columbus, OH.

Hawley, W., & Valli, L. (1999). The essentials of effective professional development: A new consensus. In L. Darling-Hammond & G. Sykes (Eds.), *Teaching as the learning profession* (pp. 127–150). San Francisco: Jossey-Bass.

Hiebert, J., & Stigler, J. W. (2000). A proposal for improving classroom teaching: Lessons from the TIMSS Video Study. *Elementary School Journal, 101,* 3–20.

Hoffman, J. (2001, May). *Providing exemplary professional development for quality literacy instruction in schools.* Presentation at the Literacy Specialist Conference, Columbus, OH.

International Reading Association. (2004a). *Standards for reading professionals: Revised 2003.* Newark, DE: Author.

International Reading Association. (2004b). *The role and qualifications of the reading coach in the United States: A position statement of the International Reading Association.* Newark: DE: Author.

International Reading Association (Author) and Lamplight Media (Producer). (2003). *Reciprocal teaching strategies at work: Improving reading comprehension, grades 2–6* [Video]. Newark, DE: International Reading Association.

International Reading Association and the National Association for the Education of Young Children. (1998). *Learning to read and write: Developmentally appropriate practices for young children.* Newark, DE: Authors.

Joyce, B., & Showers, B. (1995). *Student achievement through staff development: Fundamentals of school renewal.* White Plains, NY: Longman.

King, P. M., & Kitchener, K. S. (2004). Reflective judgment: Theory and research on the development of epistemic assumptions through adulthood. *Educational Psychologist, 39,* 5–18.

Krathwohl, D. R. (2002). A revision of Bloom's taxonomy: An overview. *Theory into Practice, 41,* 212–218.

Kraus, R. (1971). *Leo the late bloomer.* New York: Windmill Books.

Lareau, A. (2000). *Home advantage.* Charlotte, NC: Rowman & Littlefield.

Learning First Alliance. (2000). *Every child reading: A professional development guide.* Washington, DC: Author.

Lenhart, L., Brown, R., Roskos, K., Krosnick, L., Rosemary, C., & McGloin, D. (2005, April). *Design dilemmas and implementation challenges of large-scale online professional development in effective reading instruction.* Paper presented at the annual meeting of the American Educational Research Association, Montreal, Canada.

Loucks-Horsley, S., Hewson, P., Love, N., & Stiles, K. (1998). *Designing professional development for teachers of science and mathematics.* Thousand Oaks, CA: Corwin Press.

McAninch, A. R. (1993). *Teacher thinking and the case method.* New York: Teachers College Press.

McKenna, M., & Stahl, S. A. (2003). *Assessment for reading instruction,* New York: Guilford Press.

McMahon, S. I., Raphael, T. E., Goatley, V. J., & Pardo, L. S. (1997). *Book club connection.* New York: Teachers College Press.

Minarik, E. (1957). *Little bear.* New York: HarperTrophy.

Moats, L. (2002). *A blueprint for professional development for teachers of reading knowledge, skills, and learning activities.* Washington, DC: United States Department of Education. The Secretary's Reading Leadership Academy.

National Council for Accreditation of Teacher Education. (2004). *Approved curriculum guidelines: IRA advanced reading education guidelines.* Washington, DC: Author.

National Partnership for Excellence and Accountability in Teaching. (2001). Retrieved July 19, 2005, from http://ed-web3.educ.msu.edu/npeat/

National Reading Panel. (2000). *Report of the National Reading Panel: Teaching children to read: An evidence-based assessment of the scientific research literature on reading and its implications for reading instruction* (NIH No. 00-4769). Washington, DC: National Institute of Child Health and Human Development.

National Research Council. (2000). *Preventing reading difficulties in young children.* Washington, DC: National Academy Press.

National Staff Development Council. (2001). *Standards for staff development.* Retrieved from www.nsdc.org

Ogle, D. S. (1986). K–W–L group instructional strategy. In A. S. Palincsar, D. S. Ogle, B. F. Jones, & E. G. Carr (Eds.), *Teaching reading as thinking* (Teleconference Resource Guide, pp. 11–17). Alexandria, VA: Association for Supervision and Curriculum Development.

Ohio Department of Education. (1999). *Ohio Literacy Initiative: A basic framework for literacy development.* Columbus, OH: Author.

Ohio Department of Education. (2002). *Academic content standards: K–12 English language arts*. Columbus, OH: Author.

Perkins, D. (1998). What is understanding? In M. Wiske (Ed.), *Teaching for understanding: Linking research with practice* (pp. 39–58). San Francisco: Jossey-Bass.

Phelps, G., & Schilling, S. (2004). Developing measures of content knowledge for teaching reading. *Elementary School Journal, 105*, 31–48.

Putnam, R. T., & Borko, H. (2000). What do new views of knowledge and thinking have to say about research on teacher learning? *Educational Researcher, 29*, 4–15.

Randi, J., & Zeichner, K. M. (2004). New visions of teacher professional development. In M. Smylie & D. Miretzky (Eds.), *Developing the teacher workforce: 103rd Yearbook of the National Society for the Study of Education* (pp. 180–227). Chicago: National Society for the Study of Education.

Read, C. (1971). Pre-school children's knowledge of English phonology. *Harvard Educational Review, 41*, 1–34.

Richardson, V. (1994). Conducting research on practice. *Educational Researcher, 23*(5), 5–10.

Robelen, E. W. (2003, December). 13 nominated to new panel overseeing federal education research. *Education Week, 23*(15). Retrieved from http://www.edweek.org/ew/articles/2003/12/10/15nbes.h23. html?qs=new_panel_overseeing

Rose, D. H., & Meyer, A. (2002). *Teaching every student in the digital age: Universal design for learning*. Alexandria, VA: Association for Supervision and Curriculum Development.

Rosemary, C. A. (2005). Teacher Learning Instrument: A metacognitive tool for improving literacy teaching. In S. Israel, C. C. Block, & K. Kinnucan-Welsch (Eds.), *Metacognition in literacy learning: Theory, assessment, instruction, and professional development* (pp. 351–371). Mahwah, NJ: Erlbaum.

Rosemary, C. A., Freppon, P., & Kinnucan-Welsch, K. (with Grogan, P., Feist-Willis, J., Zimmerman, B., Campbell, L., Cobb, J., et al.). (2002). Improving literacy teaching through structured collaborative inquiry in classroom and university clinical settings. In D. Schallert, C. Fairbanks, J. Worthy, B. Maloch, & J. Hoffman (Eds.), *51st yearbook of the National Reading Conference* (pp. 368–382). Oak Creek, WI: National Reading Conference.

Roskos, K. A. (2000). *Teaching reading and writing: A core curriculum for educators* (produced in cooperation with faculty from John Carroll University, Kent State University, Ohio University, Ohio State University, University of Cincinnati, University of Toledo, and Youngstown State University). Columbus: Ohio Department of Education.

Roskos, K. A., Christie, J. F., & Richgels, D. J. (2003). The essentials of early literacy instruction. *Young Children, 58*, 52–60.

Roskos, K. A., & Neuman, S. B. (2001). Environment and its influences for early literacy teaching. In S. B. Neuman & D. K. Dickinson (Eds.), *The handbook of early literacy research* (Vol. 1, pp. 281–294). New York: Guilford Press.

Roskos, K. A., & Vukelich, C. (1998). How do practicing teachers grow and learn as professionals? In S. B. Neuman & K. A. Roskos (Eds.), *Children achieving: Best practices in early literacy* (pp. 250–271). Newark, DE: International Reading Association.

Sandoval, W. A., Deneroff, V., & Franke, M. (2002, April). *Teacher identity and practice in inquiry based science*. Paper presented at the annual meeting of the American Educational Research Association, New Orleans, LA.

Saunders, W., & Goldenberg, C. (1996). Four primary teachers work to define constructivism and teacher-directed learning: Implications for teacher assessment. *Elementary School Journal, 97*, 139–161.

Schickedanz, J. (1999). *Much more than the ABCs: The early stages of reading and writing*. Washington, DC: National Association for the Education of Young Children.

Schon, D. (1987). *Educating the reflective practitioner*. San Francisco: Jossey-Bass.

Scieszka, J. (1995). *The true story of the three little pigs by A. Wolf*. New York: Dutton Books.

Shaywitz, B., Pugh, K. R., Jenner, A. R., Fulbright, R. K., Fletcher, J. M., Gore, J. C., et al. (2000). The neurobiology of reading and reading disability (dyslexia). In M. Kamil, P. Mosenthal, P. Pearson, & R. Barr (Eds.), *Handbook of reading research* (Vol. 3, pp. 229–249). Mahwah, NJ: Erlbaum.

Shonkoff, J. P., & Phillips, D. A. (Eds.). (2004). *From neurons to neighborhoods: The science of early childhood development*. Washington, DC: National Academy Press, Committee on Integrating the Science of Early Childhood Development.

Shulman, L. (1986). Those who understand: Knowledge growth in teaching. *Educational Researcher, 15*(2), 4–14.

Shulman, L. (1987). Knowledge and teaching: Foundations of the new reform. *Harvard Educational Review, 57,* 1–22.

Smith, M. W., & Dickinson, D. K. (2002). *Early language and literacy classroom observation toolkit.* Baltimore: Brookes.

Snow, C. E., Burns, S. M., & Griffin, P. (Eds.). (1998). *Preventing reading difficulties in young children.* Washington, DC: National Academy Press.

Snow, C. E., Griffin, P., & Burns, S. M. (2005). *Knowledge to support the teaching of reading: Preparing teachers for a changing world.* San Francisco: Jossey-Bass.

Sparks, D. (2005). Explain, inspire, and lead. *Journal of Staff Development, 26,* 50–53.

Sprinthall, N. A., Reiman, A. J., & Thies-Sprinthall, L. (1996). Teacher professional development. In J. Sikula, T. Buttery, & E. Guyton (Eds.), *Handbook of research on teacher education* (2nd ed., pp. 666–703). New York: Macmillan Library Reference.

Staal, L. (2000). The story face: An adaptation of story mapping that incorporates visualization and discovery learning to enhance reading and writing. *The Reading Teacher, 54,* 27–31.

Stanovich, K. (1994). Romance and reality. *The Reading Teacher, 47,* 280–291.

Stanovich, P. J., & Stanovich, K. E. (2003). *Using research and reason in education: How teachers can use scientifically based research to make curricular and instructional decisions.* Jessup, MD: Ed Pubs.

Stauffer, R. (1975). *Directing the reading–thinking process.* New York: Harper & Row.

Strickland. D., & Shanahan, T. (2004). Laying the groundwork for literacy. *Educational Leadership, 61,* 74–77.

Sykes, G. (1996). Reform of and as professional development. *Phi Delta Kappan, 77,* 464–467.

Sykes, G. (1999). Introduction: Teaching and the learning profession. In L. Darling-Hammond & G. Sykes (Eds.), *Teaching as the learning profession: Handbook of policy and practice* (pp. xv–xxiii). San Francisco: Jossey-Bass.

Tharp, R. G., & Gallimore, R. (1988). *Rousing minds to life: Teaching, learning, and schooling in social context.* New York: Cambridge University Press.

The LS Exchange, Volumes 1–21. (2000–2005). University Heights, OH: John Carroll University.

Tower, C. (2000). Questions that matter: Preparing elementary students for the inquiry process. *The Reading Teacher, 53,* 550–557.

Trubowitz, S. (2000). Predictable problems in achieving large-scale change. *Phi Delta Kappan, 82,* 166–168.

Ulrich, D. (1997). *Human resource champions.* Cambridge, MA: Harvard Business School Press.

U.S. Department of Education. (2001). *No Child Left Behind.* Jessup, MD: Author.

Vygotsky, L. (1978). *Mind in society: The development of psychological processes.* Cambridge, MA: Harvard University Press.

Wagner, R. B. (1989). *Accountability in education: A philosophical inquiry.* New York: Routledge.

Westcott, N. B. (1987). *Raffi songs to read: Down by the bay.* Needham Heights, MA: Silver Burdett Ginn.

Wiggins, G., & McTighe, J. (1998). *Understanding by design.* Alexandria, VA: Association for Supervision and Curriculum Development.

Wilson, S. M., & Berne, J. (1999). Teacher learning and the acquisition of professional knowledge: An examination of research on contemporary professional development. *Review of Research in Education, 24,* 173–209.

Wolfersberger, M. E., Reutzel, D. R., Sudweeks, R., & Fawson, P. C. (2004). Developing and validating the classroom literacy environmental profile (CLEP): A tool for examining the "print richness" of early childhood and elementary classrooms. *Journal of Literacy Research, 36*(2), 211–272.

Zull, J. E. (2002). *The art of changing the brain: Enriching the practice of teaching by exploring the biology of learning.* Sterling, VA: Stylus.

Zull, J. E. (2004, May). *Emotion, brain, learning, motivation.* Presentation at the Literacy Specialist Conference, Cambridge, OH.

Index